The Best of Casual Pizza Oven Cooking

PIZZERIA

Produced by
WELDON OWEN INC.
Chief Executive Officer: John Owen
President: Terry Newell
Publisher/Vice President: Wendely Harvey
Managing Editor: Lisa Chaney Atwood
Project Coordinator: Judith Dunham
Consulting Editor: Norman Kolpas
Copy Editor: Sharon Silva
Design: Patty Hill
Production Director: Stephanie Sherman
Production Manager: Jen Dalton
Production Editor: Sarah Lemas
Co-Editions Director: Derek Barton
Food Photography: Peter Johnson
Assistant Food Photographer: Mil Truscott
Food Stylist: Janice Baker
Assistant Food Stylist: Liz Nolan
Half-Title Illustration: Martha Anne Booth
Chapter Opener Illustrations: Miriam Fabbri
Glossary Illustrations: Alice Harth
Photo Research: Amelia Ames Hill

Production by Kyodo Printing Co.
(S'pore) Pte Ltd
Printed in Singapore

Original edition printed in 1997.
This edition printed in 2004.

10 9 8 7 6 5 4 3 2 1

ISBN 1-74089-533-9

Cataloging-in-Publication data is available.

A Note on Weights and Measures:
All recipes include customary U.S. and metric measurements.
Metric conversions are based on a standard developed for these
books and have been rounded off. Actual weights may vary.

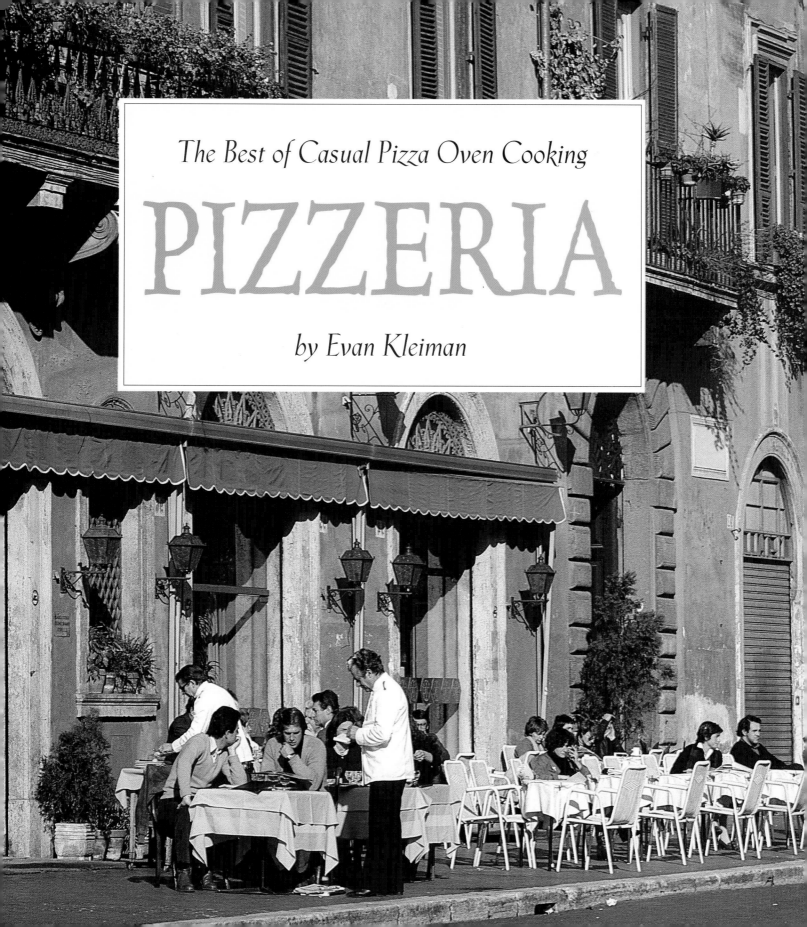

The Best of Casual Pizza Oven Cooking

PIZZERIA

by Evan Kleiman

Contents

Introduction 7

Antipasti 17

Pizzas and Calzone 39

Focaccia and Panini 71

Light Meals 87

Desserts 109

Introduction

The aroma usually grabs you before you ever set eyes on a pizzeria. The air is filled with the scent of tomatoes, garlic, herbs, baking bread and bubbling cheese. Irresistibly, you are drawn to the source.

Inside, the wondrous smells are joined by the convivial hum of contented diners, punctuated by brisk, jocular shouts as orders are passed from waiter to pizza chef. The interior of the pizzeria is usually simple and spare, almost ascetic. Gleaming terrazzo, marble or tile floors may be strewn with a few handfuls of sawdust to catch drips of oil or sauce. Tables are small squares of streaky white marble or thick slabs of wood. Wainscoting of the same materials surrounds the dining room walls.

Inevitably lured back to the food, you notice that other specialties share the stage with the array of pizzas: simple salads and varied antipasti; sauced and baked pastas; focaccia cut into wedges or squares, or split in half and filled to make *panini;* roasted chicken and other rustic main dishes; and a selection of classic Italian desserts. The food, the sights, the sounds, the aromas—all conspire to make you feel comfortably, casually at home, among family. This is what brings you back, again and again, to a great pizzeria.

Pizzeria History

The roots of the modern pizza may be traced back to the first century A.D., but it wasn't until sometime after the arrival in Naples of the tomato from the New World in the sixteenth century that pizzas began to resemble the food we know today. Soon after tomatoes joined the dough, the modern pizzeria had its humble beginnings in the streets of Naples as a way to provide quick, basic food—literally, the daily bread—to hungry Neapolitan working people. Small rooms were cut into the city's venerable stone walls to house beehive-shaped ovens in which *pizzaioli,* or "pizza makers," would bake disks of dough, topped simply with tomatoes, a drizzle of olive oil and some oregano. Hot from the oven, the pizzas would be folded in half, tucked into a sheet from yesterday's newspaper and sold over the counter to be eaten out of hand in the street.

The late nineteenth and early twentieth centuries saw many workers leave Naples in search of better lives in America, and the *pizzaioli* brought their talent and recipes with them. They began their American careers working in Italian bakeries, where pizza first appeared as focaccia, or "pan pizza," with a thicker, more breadlike crust resembling pizzas of the south. Upon saving a bit of money, these new immigrants opened their own pizza shops, offering over-the-counter service like their ancestors in the old country.

The Great Depression of the 1930s saw many such pizzerias open, providing reasonably priced sustenance to struggling families. But it was with the return of the GIs from Europe after World War II that pizza began to develop the extraordinary following it has today. As pizzerias gained in popularity in the late 1950s and early 1960s, they grew in size, adding tables and amplifying the menu with simple regional Italian specialties that might appeal to a broader clientele. In the 1970s, an explosion of interest in cooking influenced by fresh ingredients and the traditions of different European and Asian cuisines brought still more variety to the pizzeria, as pizzas were served with ever-more-creative combinations of sauces, toppings and cheeses. As cooking and eating habits change, so does the adaptable pizzeria change with them.

The Pizzeria Experience

A meal at a pizzeria is slice-of-life theater. Star of the show is the *pizzaiolo,* clad in a low, square cap of white cotton, a white T-shirt and trousers swathed in a white apron. Always onstage near the oven, he enjoys a lively banter with customers who watch him work his magic.

The *pizzaiolo* performs his acts of culinary conjuring on a work surface of marble, to keep the dough cool. Surrounding him are containers holding all the colors, textures, tastes and scents that will give character to

his creations: scarlet cherry or plum tomatoes; mounds of opaque fresh mozzarella, floating in whey; lustrous, dark, briny olives; silvery fillets of anchovy; bouquets of basil and oregano; big, salt-encrusted capers; freshly ground black peppercorns and red chilies; and large crystals of coarse salt. A simple metal can with a beaklike spout holds fragrant extra-virgin olive oil, to be drizzled onto each disk as a finishing touch.

The *pizzaiolo* goes to work, often sending a round of dough whirling off his fists into the air as he stretches it out to the ideal circular dimensions and thinness. While you watch this now-signature feat of pizza making, you might choose to whet your appetite with a mixed green salad or a salad of tomatoes and fresh mozzarella, or some antipasti cooked in the pizza oven earlier that day. Or the pizza might be an appetizer that

you share with friends or family before proceeding to a pasta dish or a plump roasted chicken. With the varied menus of so many pizzerias today, you have the option of bypassing the legendary pie altogether— perhaps making a light lunch of a simple *panino,* or "sandwich." Desserts, too, are there should you want them. Tempting though they are, you're unlikely to be pressured into ordering them. For that matter, you might stop into the pizzeria for nothing more than dessert and coffee at the end of an evening.

A good pizzeria remains spiritually linked to the streetside counters of old Naples. Whatever you choose to order, however long you linger, the show goes on, ready to sweep you happily along with it.

Bringing the Pizzeria Home

Plain white plates or other rustic dishes and serving pieces, along with monochromatic or checkered napkins and tablecloths or placemats in coarse linen, cotton or even paper, will evoke the pizzeria's simplicity and humble roots. For the pasta recipes in this book, use the wide, shallow bowls Italians customarily prefer for serving this staple.

Special pizza-making equipment can help you achieve authentic results. Intense heat and direct contact of the dough with the heat source are crucial to create a great pizza, with a well-crisped crust that finishes baking in the same time it takes the topping

to cook. Pizza stones or tiles transform a home oven into an environment that more closely resembles a traditional bread oven. Place them in a cold oven, following the manufacturer's directions and letting them preheat as the oven does. Easiest to find, and most readily adaptable to both gas and electric ovens, are round pizza stones that are placed on an oven rack set at the lowest level. You can also find square stones or unglazed tiles that sit directly on the oven floor and don't need to be removed to accommodate other cookware.

A pizza peel, a wide wooden spatula with a long handle, makes sliding a pizza into the oven a safe and simple task. If you prefer not to invest in a peel, you can use an inverted rimless baking sheet. Some home cooks like to hang their wooden pizza peels on the wall as decoration when not in use, keeping the spirit of the pizzeria ever present in their kitchens.

Beverages

Pizzerias, by their nature, are simple places, so it is no surprise that their beverage menus are usually abbreviated offerings. The most popular *aperitivo* is probably ruby red Campari, with its mild bitterness customarily balanced by club soda (see opposite page). Punt e Mes and Cinzano are two other frequently encountered alcohol-based *aperitivi*. Among the good nonalcoholic choices are a variety of sweet syrups, such as almond-flavored *orzata* or mint-flavored *menta,* each mixed with soda water to form a sparkling, thirst-quenching drink. The not-too-sweet citrus sodas—*aranciata* (orange) and *limonata* (lemon)—are wonderfully refreshing sipped not only at the start of a meal but also along with pizza. A small bowl of green and black olives and a second bowl of mixed red and green *peperoncini* marinated in extra-virgin olive oil, or sometimes an assortment of antipasti, are often set out for nibbling.

Wine and Beer

Wine pairs naturally with pizza, pasta and simple roast meats. In nearly every sit-down pizzeria, both red and white wines are decanted into glass or ceramic carafes or into bottles, from which customers pour their choice into short, faceted tumblers. A pizzeria located near a wine district might also serve *un litro,* a one-liter carafe of a local vintage.

In a casual establishment, the owner sometimes decants bulk wine into clean, empty wine bottles from which the labels have been removed. A single bottle may then circulate to more than one table over the course of an evening. To keep track of how much money a customer owes for wine, the proprietor marks the level of the wine on the bottle with a grease pencil before delivering it to a second table. At an upscale pizzeria, bottled wines from outside the area are offered in addition to regionally produced ones. They often include one or two Chiantis and one or two lightly chilled whites, perhaps Pinot Grigio or Tocai Friulano, all of them perfect for chasing down the strong flavors sometimes found atop pizzas. The most exciting of the bottled wines are the new *vini da tavola.* These special table wines are produced by a new generation of wine makers who are experimenting with different grape varieties and vinifying and barreling techniques. Tuscan wine makers are among the first to have flirted with these innovative stylings, and thus many of the fine, new table wines are called super-Tuscans. Their rich, complex flavors are ideal for pairing with a spicy pizza, a simple pasta or an herb-rubbed roast chicken.

For some pizza aficionados, a cold beer—whether from a bottle or *alla spina,* "on tap"—is the best choice in a pizzeria. Large bottles of regional beers are on the beverage list of more informal pizza purveyors. An upscale pizzeria often has a good selection of imported beers and ales as well. The beer from a bottle is poured into short, plain glasses, the beer on tap into tall glasses.

After–Dinner Drinks

A variety of beverages make the perfect finish to a pizzeria meal, including Sambuca, Fernet Branca, Averna and grappa. Grappa, a popular Italian *digestivo,* has been appreciated for its medicinal and festive qualities since the twelfth century. It is distilled from the grape mash left over from wine making. White, straw or amber in color and possessing an intensely herbaceous "nose," grappa has an alcohol level of 40 to 50 percent, which ensures imbibers that the meal will end with a strong kick.

The owner of an informal pizzeria frequently decants grappa from a large demijohn into two-liter bottles filled with an assortment of herbs and citrus peels. A bottle of this aromatic spirit is plunked down on the table with a stack of shot glasses to be enjoyed by anyone who wishes to partake.

In establishments that do not serve spirits, the dessert drink of choice is generally Vin Santo, which has an appealing nutty flavor and sweet-dry finish. This Tuscan dessert wine is usually served in large shot glasses, accompanied with a basket of small biscotti for dipping.

The arrival of espresso or cappuccino signals the end of the repast. A small ceramic cup of rich, black espresso is the traditional finish to all Italian meals. *Caffè corretto,* coffee "corrected" with a shot of grappa, is requested by those who wish the excess of the meal to continue. Cappuccino is the richest way to cap off a pizzeria visit—the frothy milk lifting high above the rim of a stout coffee cup.

CAMPARI AND SODA

The quintessential Italian aperitivo was invented by a Milanese, Gaspare Campari, in the 1860s. It is a secret mixture of herbs, bitter orange peel and other aromatic substances steeped in an alcohol base. The resulting slightly bitter flavor, combined with club soda on ice and given a hint of citrus, whets the appetite for the meal to come.

   Ice cubes
⅓ cup (3 fl oz/80 ml) Campari
⅔ cup (5 fl oz/160 ml) club soda
   Twist of lemon peel or a lime wedge

▨ Fill a tall, narrow 12–fl oz (375-ml) glass half full with ice cubes. Pour the Campari over the ice cubes. Add the club soda and stir. Garnish with a lemon twist or lime wedge.

Serves 1

Basic Recipes

Pizzeria chefs rely on a handful of essential recipes to prepare a wide variety of dishes. A recipe for classic Neapolitan pizza dough is joined by a versatile focaccia. Simple sauces, both an uncooked and a cooked tomato sauce, and a pesto, not only top pizzas but are paired with pasta and other pizza fare.

NEAPOLITAN PIZZA DOUGH

IMPASTO PER PIZZA ALLA NAPOLETANA

A Neapolitan pizza crust must be thin, but not cracker-thin as is traditional in Rome. If you prefer an extra-crisp super-thin crust, roll the dough into a round 11 inches (28 cm) in diameter rather than the 9 inches (23 cm) specified in the pizza recipes. Note that these directions make enough for 2 crusts. The pizza recipes in this book call for only half that amount. You can refrigerate the extra dough for up to 2 days or freeze for up to 1 month, or double the topping ingredients in the recipes and make 2 pizzas.

1½ teaspoons active dry yeast
¼   cup (2 fl oz/60 ml) lukewarm water (105°F/42°C)
1½ tablespoons olive oil
½   cup (4 fl oz/125 ml) cold water
1⅔ cups (8½ oz/265 g) unbleached all-purpose (plain) flour, plus flour for kneading
¾   teaspoon salt

◉ In a large mixing bowl, stir the yeast into the lukewarm water. Let stand until creamy, about 10 minutes. Stir in the olive oil and the cold water, and then whisk in ½ cup (2½ oz/75 g) of the flour and the salt, stirring until smooth. Stir in the remaining flour, ½ cup (2½ oz/75 g) at a time, until the dough comes together in a rough mass.

◉ On a lightly floured work surface, knead the dough until smooth and velvety, 8–10 minutes. It will be soft. Cover loosely with a kitchen towel and let rest for 15 minutes.

◉ Divide into 2 equal portions, knead briefly, then roll each portion into a smooth, tight round ball. To use the dough immediately, sprinkle a little flour on the work surface and set the balls on it. Cover them with a kitchen towel and let rise for 1 hour, then stretch and top the dough as directed in each recipe.

◉ You may also store one or both balls of dough until ready to use. For short-term storage and for a slow rise resulting in more flavor, place the dough balls on a small baking pan lined with a kitchen towel, cover them with a second towel and refrigerate for up to 48 hours; remove from the refrigerator and let stand at room temperature for 10–15 minutes before forming the pizza. For longer storage, slip each flour-dusted ball into a plastic freezer bag, seal tightly and freeze for up to 1 month. Before use, place the frozen dough in a lightly oiled bowl, cover loosely with plastic wrap, and let thaw overnight in the refrigerator or for about 2 hours at room temperature. The thawed dough should be puffy and soft to the touch.

Makes enough for two 9-inch (23-cm) pizza crusts

HERB-FLAVORED FOCACCIA

FOCACCIA ALLE ERBE

Focaccia dough is softer than pizza dough, yielding a nearly cakelike interior once it is baked. Baking the focaccia in cake pans results in rounds 1½ inches (4 cm) thick—perfect for pairing with an unlimited variety of panino *fillings or slicing to serve plain as an accompaniment to any meal. If you prefer a crisp crust, drizzle the dough with a generous amount of olive oil before baking. For a soft crust, brush the focaccia with olive oil immediately upon removing it from the oven.*

2½   teaspoons (1 package) active dry yeast

1   cup (8 fl oz/240 ml) lukewarm water (105°F/42°C)

2   tablespoons olive oil

2   cups (10 oz/310 g) unbleached all-purpose (plain) flour, plus flour for kneading

1   teaspoon salt

2   tablespoons chopped fresh chives

1   tablespoon chopped fresh thyme

1½   teaspoons finely chopped fresh rosemary
     Extra-virgin olive oil for brushing
     Coarse salt

◈ In a large mixing bowl, stir the yeast into ¼ cup (2 fl oz/60 ml) of the lukewarm water. Let stand until creamy, about 10 minutes. Stir in the remaining ¾ cup (6 fl oz/180 ml) lukewarm water and the olive oil. Add 1 cup (5 oz/155 g) of the flour and the salt and whisk until smooth. Add the chives, thyme and rosemary and mix well, then stir in the remaining 1 cup (5 oz/155 g) flour, ½ cup (2½ oz/75 g) at a time, until the dough comes together in a rough mass.

◈ On a lightly floured work surface, knead the dough until smooth and velvety, 8–10 minutes. It will be soft. Lightly oil a bowl, place the dough in it and turn the dough to coat with oil. Cover the bowl with plastic wrap and put in a warm place to rise until doubled in bulk, about 1½ hours.

◈ Divide the dough into 2 equal portions and knead briefly. The dough is now ready to be stretched and topped as directed in the recipes or baked plain as directed below. You may also store the dough, as directed for the Neapolitan pizza dough opposite, until ready to use. If you prefer thinner, more resilient focaccia, stretch out the dough into a larger pan.

◈ If plain focaccia is preferred, lightly oil two 8-inch (20-cm) cake pans. Place each portion of dough in a prepared pan and gently stretch it out to the edges, pulling it from the center outward to achieve an even thickness. If the dough springs back toward the center and is difficult to work with, cover and set it aside for 10 minutes to relax, then continue coaxing the dough out to an even thickness. Cover the pans with kitchen towels and let rise until almost doubled in bulk and very soft and puffy, about 45 minutes.

◈ Preheat an oven to 475°F (245°C). Using your fingertips, dimple the dough in several places, leaving indentations about ½ inch (12 mm) deep. Again cover the pans with towels and let rise for 20 minutes longer.

◈ Bake until golden brown and cooked through, 15–18 minutes. Remove from the oven and immediately brush the tops with a generous amount of extra-virgin olive oil, then sprinkle with coarse salt. Serve hot or at room temperature.

Makes two 8-inch (20-cm) rounds

UNCOOKED TOMATO SAUCE

SALSA DI POMODORO CRUDO

This simple sauce is the traditional topping on a Neapolitan pizza and suits a wide range of pizza preparations. It is light on the palate and fulfills its role as an undernote to pizza, allowing the additional toppings to stand out.

If you are using canned tomatoes, look for the sweetest ones you can find. Taste them out of the can and, if they are a bit too acidic, add a pinch of sugar.

8 ripe plum (Roma) tomatoes or 1 can (16 oz/500 g) plum (Roma) tomatoes with their juices
1 tablespoon extra-virgin olive oil
   Salt and freshly ground pepper

 Fit a food mill with the coarse or medium blade and place over a small mixing bowl. Pass the tomatoes through the mill into the bowl. Alternatively, use a food processor: Peel the fresh tomatoes, if using. Place the fresh or canned tomatoes in a food processor fitted with the metal blade and pulse to form a coarse purée. Add the olive oil and season to taste with salt and pepper. Use immediately, or transfer to a tightly covered container and refrigerate for up to 2 days.

Makes about 1½ cups (12 fl oz/375 ml), enough for six 9-inch (23-cm) pizzas

TOMATO-BASIL SAUCE

SALSA DI POMODORO E BASILICO

This flavorful, yet basic, sauce embodies the simple, rustic elegance of classic Italian cooking at its best. It is used in a wide range of Italian dishes, including soups, pastas, baked dishes, risotto and, of course, pizzas, to which it adds a deeper, more fully developed flavor than the uncooked tomato sauce at left.

If you find that your tomatoes lack a good balance of sweetness and acidity, add a few pinches of sugar to bring out their natural sweetness.

¼ cup (2 fl oz/60 ml) extra-virgin olive oil
2 cloves garlic, minced
12 plum (Roma) tomatoes, peeled, seeded and chopped, or 1 can (28 oz/875 g) plum (Roma) tomatoes, chopped, with their juices
8 large fresh basil leaves, coarsely chopped
   Salt and freshly ground pepper

In a large frying pan over medium heat, warm the oil. Add the garlic and sauté for a few seconds just until fragrant. Add the tomatoes and cook, stirring frequently, until they begin to break down and form a sauce, about 10 minutes.

Add the basil, season to taste with salt and pepper and raise the heat to medium-high. Cook, stirring occasionally, until the sauce thickens and is no longer watery, 15–20 minutes.

Use immediately, or transfer to a container with a tight-fitting lid and refrigerate for up to 2 days.

Makes about 2 cups (16 fl oz/500 ml)

GENOVESE PESTO

PESTO ALLA GENOVESE

Few sauces represent a season as perfectly as this summer sauce from Liguria. The distinct flavors of basil and garlic, mellowed with Italian Parmesan, give it a versatility matched by few other sauces. It can be used for pasta and pizza, spread on crostini *and* panini, *even used as a marinade for roasted meats. Vary the amount of olive oil according to your own preferences: use less for a light, fluffy texture and more for a denser, heavier and more flavorful sauce.*

¼   cup (1 oz/30 g) pine nuts or walnuts

2   cups (2 oz/60 g) firmly packed fresh basil leaves

4–6 cloves garlic

½–1 cup (4–8 fl oz/125–250 ml) extra-virgin olive oil

¼   cup (1 oz/30 g) freshly grated Italian Parmesan cheese

¼   cup (1 oz/30 g) freshly grated Italian pecorino romano cheese
     Salt and freshly ground pepper

◧ Preheat an oven to 350°F (180°C). Spread the nuts in a single layer on a baking sheet. Place in the oven until lightly toasted and fragrant, about 8 minutes. Remove from the heat and let cool.

◧ In a food processor fitted with the metal blade or in a blender, combine the basil and garlic and pulse until finely chopped, scraping down the sides of the bowl as necessary. With the motor running, add ½ cup (4 fl oz/125 ml) of the olive oil in a slow, steady stream. Scatter the cheeses over the top, then pulse until the cheeses are absorbed. Again with the motor running, slowly add the remaining oil and process until creamy.

◧ Season to taste with salt and pepper, add the nuts and pulse just until the nuts are coarsely chopped. Use immediately, or pour into a container and top with a thin layer of olive oil. Cover tightly and refrigerate for up to 4 days.

Makes about 2 cups (16 fl oz/500 ml)

Antipasti

The contemporary sit-down pizzeria would not be complete without an abundant display of antipasti to whet customers' appetites. Tender eggplant crosshatched with grill marks, strips of scarlet roasted bell peppers, delicate slices or balls of fresh mozzarella cheese and creamy white beans flecked with the herbs from a marinade are among the classic Italian antipasti on the menu.

An innovative pizzeria chef will often reinterpret favorite antipasti in new ways, perhaps rolling eggplant slices around fresh goat cheese or wrapping mozzarella in marinated grape leaves and searing them on a grill. A few salads enlivened with artichokes or sautéed mushrooms cater to today's interest in light, fresh foods. Or an unusual new dish such as bite-sized sandwiches made with polenta might appear among the antipasti selections.

Such creations underscore that few courses of a meal hold the potential to inspire both chef and appetite as do the antipasti. Because portions are meant to be small, flavors can be big and bold to make the maximum first impression. Abundant herbs and sharp, piquant condiments are joined with the freshest of market vegetables or the finest cheeses. Every trip to the market can yield new and delicious combinations for cook and hungry diner alike.

Deep-fried Polenta-Gorgonzola Sandwiches

In Italy, pizza vendors sometimes offer bite-sized rectangles of deep-fried polenta in addition to a regular assortment of simply prepared pizzas. In this upscale version of the crispy Italian snack, creamy, pungent Gorgonzola is sandwiched between thin slices of golden polenta, then deep-fried.

GORGONZOLA FILLING

1¼ lb (625 g) spinach, tough stems removed

¼ lb (125 g) Gorgonzola cheese, crumbled

Pinch of freshly grated nutmeg

Salt and freshly ground pepper

POLENTA

2 cups (16 fl oz/500 ml) water

2 cups (16 fl oz/500 ml) chicken stock

1 teaspoon salt

1 cup (5 oz/155 g) polenta or coarsely ground yellow cornmeal

2 tablespoons unsalted butter

⅓ cup (1½ oz/45 g) freshly grated Italian Parmesan cheese

1 ball fresh mozzarella, ½ lb (250 g), cut into slices ½ inch (12 mm) thick, then torn into quarters

Vegetable oil for deep-frying

1 cup (5 oz/155 g) all-purpose (plain) flour

1 egg

½ cup (4 fl oz/125 ml) water

1 cup (4 oz/125 g) fine dried bread crumbs

Tomato-basil sauce *(recipe on page 14),* warmed

◧ To make the filling, rinse the spinach, but do not dry. Place in a saucepan over medium-low heat, cover and cook, turning occasionally, until wilted, 2–4 minutes. Drain the spinach and squeeze to remove the liquid. Chop coarsely and place in a bowl. Add the Gorgonzola, nutmeg and salt and pepper to taste. Toss to mix well.

◧ To make the polenta, in a large, heavy saucepan, combine the water, stock and salt. Bring to a simmer. Sprinkle in the polenta or cornmeal in a slow, thin stream, whisking constantly. Reduce the heat to very low and cook, stirring every 1–2 minutes, until the mixture comes away from the sides of the pan and the grains have begun to soften, 15–20 minutes total. Stir in the butter and Parmesan and remove from the heat.

◧ Rinse a 6-by-9-inch (15-by-23-cm) roasting pan with water and shake out the excess. Working quickly and using a spatula repeatedly dipped in very hot water, evenly spread half of the polenta into the pan. Spread the filling over the polenta and distribute the mozzarella evenly over the filling. Spread the remaining polenta over the filling. Cover with a kitchen towel and let rest for at least 2 hours at room temperature or for up to 24 hours in the refrigerator.

◧ To serve, cut the polenta into eighteen 1-by-3-inch (2.5-by-7.5-cm) "sandwiches." In a large, heavy saucepan, pour in vegetable oil to a depth of about 4 inches (10 cm) and heat to 375°F (190°C) on a deep-frying thermometer. Place the flour in a shallow bowl. In a second bowl, whisk together the egg and water. Place the bread crumbs in a third bowl. Ease the sandwiches out of the pan and gently dredge in the flour, coating evenly. Carefully shake off the excess, dip both sides in the egg mixture, then coat with the bread crumbs. When the oil is hot, carefully slip 6 sandwiches into the hot oil and deep-fry until deeply golden, 4–5 minutes. Nudge occasionally with a slotted spoon to ensure they brown evenly. Transfer to paper towels to drain. Repeat with the remaining sandwiches in 2 batches.

◧ Spoon a small pool of the tomato-basil sauce on each plate, place the sandwiches on top and serve at once.

Makes 18 small sandwiches; serves 6

Tuna Salad with Peppers, Green Beans and Zucchini

Most casual Italian dining spots offer a rendition of the ubiquitous tuna salad among their antipasti. Although it is common for Italian cooks to rely on canned tuna for these creations, here grilled fresh tuna is used. The salad is delicious eaten right away or marinated for up to 24 hours.

2 large, firm yellow bell peppers (capsicums)

⅔ cup (5 fl oz/160 ml) plus 2 tablespoons extra-virgin olive oil

Juice of 2 lemons

¼ cup (⅓ oz/10 g) chopped fresh oregano or 2 teaspoons dried oregano, crumbled

2 cloves garlic, minced

Salt and freshly ground pepper

Ice water

¼ lb (125 g) small, tender green beans, ends trimmed

2 small, firm zucchini (courgettes), cut in half crosswise, then cut lengthwise into thin strips

½ lb (250 g) tuna fillet, cut into thin slices

Olive oil for brushing

10 round or pear-shaped cherry tomatoes, halved

¼ cup (⅓ oz/10 g) thinly sliced fresh basil leaves

2 teaspoons capers, rinsed and drained

◙ Preheat a broiler (griller) or preheat an oven to 450°F (230°C). Arrange the peppers on a baking sheet and place in the broiler or oven. Broil (grill) or bake, turning as necessary, until the skin is charred and blistered on all sides. Alternatively, one at a time, using tongs or a fork, hold the peppers over a gas flame until charred and blistered. Immediately place the peppers in a bowl and cover tightly with plastic wrap. Let steam until cool, about 15 minutes. Using your fingers, peel off the charred skin, then pull out and discard the stem and seeds. Cut in half lengthwise and trim away any seeds and tough white ribs. Cut each pepper lengthwise into thin strips.

◙ Prepare a fire in a charcoal grill or preheat a ridged stove-top griddle until very hot.

◙ In a small bowl, whisk together the ⅔ cup (5 fl oz/160 ml) extra-virgin olive oil, lemon juice, oregano, garlic and salt and pepper to taste. Set aside.

◙ Bring a saucepan three-fourths full of lightly salted water to a boil. Have ready a large bowl three-fourths full of ice water. Add the green beans to the boiling water, blanch for 1 minute, then drain and plunge them into the

ice water to stop the cooking and preserve the color. Transfer to a colander to drain well. Set aside.

◙ In a sauté pan over medium heat, warm the 2 tablespoons extra-virgin olive oil. Add the zucchini and sauté, stirring occasionally and regulating the heat so that the strips do not burn, until tender and golden brown, about 5 minutes. Using a slotted spoon, transfer to paper towels to drain briefly.

◙ Lightly brush the tuna slices with olive oil and season to taste with salt and pepper. Place the tuna on the grill rack about 8 inches (20 cm) above the fire or on the griddle and cook, turning once, until firm and cooked through, 3–5 minutes total. Remove from the rack or griddle and, when cool enough to handle, gently break into large pieces.

◙ In a large bowl, combine the bell peppers, green beans, zucchini, tomatoes, basil and capers. Whisk the dressing briefly, then drizzle over all. Toss gently to coat the vegetables evenly. Add the tuna and toss again gently to mix. Serve immediately, or cover and refrigerate for up to 24 hours.

Serves 6–8

Artichoke and Mushroom Salad

One of Rome's venerable salads is a rustic combination of raw artichoke hearts and curls of Parmesan cheese. In this updated version of that classic, the artichokes are cooked together with shiitake mushrooms and served on tender greens.

½ cup (4 fl oz/125 ml) plus 1 tablespoon extra-virgin olive oil

16 baby artichokes, about 1 lb (500 g), trimmed *(see glossary, page 124)* and halved lengthwise

4 cloves garlic, minced

4 tablespoons (⅓ oz/10 g) coarsely chopped fresh flat-leaf (Italian) parsley

2 tablespoons coarsely chopped fresh basil
  Juice of 1 lemon

½ cup (4 fl oz/125 ml) water
  Salt and freshly ground pepper

½ lb (250 g) fresh shiitake mushrooms, stems removed, sliced

¼ lb (125 g) mixed baby greens (about 4 cups/4 oz/125 g loosely packed)
  Extra-virgin olive oil for drizzling, optional

¼ lb (125 g) wedge Italian Parmesan cheese
  Lemon wedges

In a sauté pan just large enough to hold all the artichokes in a single layer, heat the ½ cup (4 fl oz/125 ml) olive oil over medium-high heat. Add the artichokes and sauté, turning occasionally with tongs and regulating the heat so that the artichoke halves do not burn, until golden brown and slightly crusty, about 10 minutes.

Add half of the garlic, parsley and basil and sauté for another several seconds until the aroma of the garlic is released. Add the lemon juice and water and deglaze the pan by stirring to loosen any browned bits stuck to the pan bottom. Reduce the heat to low, cover and braise the artichokes until the bases are tender when pierced with a sharp knife, about 5 minutes longer. Using a slotted spoon, remove the artichokes from the pan and set aside; keep warm. Raise the heat to high and boil the braising liquid until reduced by half, 3–5 minutes. Remove from the heat and set aside.

In another sauté pan over medium-low heat, warm the remaining 1 tablespoon olive oil. Add the shiitakes and the remaining garlic, parsley and basil. Sauté, stirring occasionally, until tender, 6–8 minutes. Remove from the heat.

Place the mixed greens in a large, shallow salad bowl. Top with the warm artichokes and shiitakes. Drizzle with a little olive oil, if desired, and the reserved braising liquid. Using a vegetable peeler, shave long curls of cheese over the top. Serve with lemon wedges.

Serves 4–6

Sweet Pepper Pinwheels with Olive Salad

Many pizzerias offer menu specials comprising a creative assortment of ingredients already on hand for pizza making. In these appetizers, roasted red peppers are the centerpiece. For convenience, you may prefer to use one of the excellent brands of firm, meaty roasted peppers packed in jars.

OLIVE SALAD

10   large green olives, pitted and coarsely chopped

20   Kalamata olives or other brine-cured black olives, pitted and coarsely chopped

1   tender celery stalk from the heart of the bunch, trimmed and minced

¼   cup (⅓ oz/10 g) coarsely chopped fresh flat-leaf (Italian) parsley

1   clove garlic, minced

2   tablespoons extra-virgin olive oil

1   tablespoon red wine vinegar
     Freshly ground pepper

PEPPER PINWHEELS

4   large, smooth red bell peppers (capsicums)
     Juice of 1 lemon

4   cloves garlic, crushed

⅓   cup (½ oz/15 g) chopped fresh basil
     Salt and freshly ground pepper

8   thin slices Black Forest ham

8   thin slices provolone cheese
     Extra-virgin olive oil for drizzling

     Lemon wedges

▣ To make the olive salad, in a bowl, combine the green olives, Kalamata or other black olives, celery, parsley, garlic, olive oil, vinegar and pepper to taste. Toss to mix well. Cover and refrigerate for at least 2 hours or for up to 24 hours to blend the flavors.

▣ To make the pepper pinwheels, preheat a broiler (griller) or preheat an oven to 450°F (230°C). Arrange the peppers on a baking sheet and place in the broiler or oven. Broil (grill) or bake, turning with tongs as necessary, until the skin is charred and blistered on all sides. Alternatively, one at a time, using tongs or a fork, hold the peppers over a gas flame until charred and blistered. Immediately place the peppers in a bowl and cover tightly with plastic wrap. Let steam until cool, about 15 minutes. Using your fingers, peel off the charred skin, then pull out and discard the stem and seeds. Cut each pepper in half and trim away any tough white ribs. Trim each half into a neat rectangle for easy rolling. Gather together all of the trimmings, mince them and add to the olive salad.

▣ Place the peppers in a bowl, sprinkle with the lemon juice and mix with the garlic cloves, basil and salt and pepper to taste. Cover and let marinate at room temperature for 1–2 hours.

▣ Discard the garlic cloves from the pepper mixture. Lay each pepper piece, smooth side down, on a work surface. Trim the ham and provolone slices into shapes similar to the pepper pieces. Lay a slice of ham atop each pepper piece and top with a slice of provolone. Starting from a short end, roll up each pepper stack tightly. Cover and refrigerate until ready to serve.

▣ Just before serving, using a sharp knife, cut each roll crosswise into 4 pinwheels. Arrange the pinwheels on a platter or on individual plates and drizzle with a little olive oil. Garnish with spoonfuls of the olive salad and lemon wedges. Serve immediately.

Serves 4–6

Mixed Green Salad

The traditional Italian way of dressing a salad is simple: First coarse salt to taste is sprinkled over the greens. Then a liberal amount of oil is drizzled over them, followed by a parsimonious amount of vinegar. The whole is then tossed vigorously. Let your taste buds be your guide.

1 head romaine (cos) lettuce, pale inner leaves only

1 head red-leaf lettuce

¼ small head red cabbage, core removed and finely shredded

2 carrots, peeled and shredded

10 cherry tomatoes, halved
Salt and freshly ground pepper

½ cup (4 fl oz/125 ml) extra-virgin olive oil, or as needed

3 tablespoons red wine vinegar, or as needed

▣ Wash and dry the lettuces well. Tear the leaves into bite-sized pieces and place in a large salad bowl. Add the red cabbage, carrots and tomatoes. Season to taste with salt and pepper.

▣ Drizzle the salad with ½ cup (4 fl oz/125 ml) olive oil. Then drizzle with 3 tablespoons vinegar. Toss together well. Taste and adjust the dressing with more oil or vinegar, if needed, then toss again and serve immediately.

Serves 4–6

Grilled Mozzarella in Grape Leaves

Anywhere grapes grow and fresh mozzarella is made, one sees these rustic little bundles rushed to tables while the wrappers are still piping hot and the cheese is creamy soft. If you have a lemon or orange tree in your yard, tuck a leaf from it inside each bundle for additional flavor and aroma.

3 balls fresh mozzarella, ½ lb (250 g) each, drained
1 jar (16 oz/500 g) grape leaves
Salt and freshly ground pepper
Vegetable oil for grilling
Tomato-basil sauce *(recipe on page 14),* warmed
Lemon wedges

▨ Soak enough raffia or kitchen string (4 yards/4 meters) or enough wooden toothpicks (20–25) to secure each mozzarella slice in a grape leaf for at least 30 minutes, then drain.

▨ Prepare a fire in a charcoal grill or preheat a ridged stove-top griddle until it is very hot. Meanwhile, cut the mozzarella into slices ½ inch (12 mm) thick. Lay them on paper towels to drain briefly.

▨ Remove the grape leaves from the jar, leaving the brine in the jar so any unused grape leaves can be returned to it. Rinse the leaves under running cold water and drain well. Using a small, sharp knife, trim away any long or tough stems from the leaves. Place 1 large leaf (or 2 overlapping smaller ones), shiny side down, on a work surface. Place 1 mozzarella slice in the center of the leaf and sprinkle to taste with salt and pepper. Bring up the sides of the leaf and wrap them around the cheese slice to enclose it completely. Tie the packets with raf-fia or kitchen string or secure with a toothpick. Repeat the process until all the mozzarella slices are wrapped.

▨ Brush some vegetable oil onto the rack of the grill or the surface of the griddle. Place the mozzarella packets on the grill rack about 6 inches (15 cm) above the fire or on the griddle and cook, turning once, until there are grill marks on the outside and the cheese has softened, 3–5 minutes total on a charcoal grill or about 5 minutes on a stove-top griddle.

▨ As soon as the cheese packets are softened and well marked from the grill, spoon some of the tomato-basil sauce onto a warmed platter or individual plates. Place the hot packets atop the sauce and garnish with the lemon wedges. Serve immediately.

Serves 4–6

Sweet-and-Sour Eggplant with Crostini

This is the queen of the Italian tradition of agrodolce, or sweet-and-sour dishes. Commonly served as an antipasto, the savory combination of eggplant, zucchini and red onion with the mild, pale yellow innermost stalks of a celery bunch is set off by the piquant flavors of capers and green olives.

1   eggplant (aubergine), unpeeled, ends trimmed and cut into ½-inch (12-mm) dice
   Salt
   Olive oil for frying, plus 2 tablespoons olive oil

2   zucchini (courgettes), ends trimmed and cut into ½-inch (12-mm) dice

1   small red (Spanish) onion, cut into ½-inch (12-mm) dice

1   celery heart, trimmed and cut crosswise into slices ½ inch (12 mm) thick

1   cup (8 fl oz/250 ml) tomato-basil sauce *(recipe on page 14)*

1   cup (5 oz/155 g) small green olives, pitted

2   cloves garlic, minced

2   tablespoons capers, rinsed and drained

¼–½   cup (2–4 oz/60–125 g) sugar

¼–½   cup (2–4 fl oz/60–125 ml) red wine vinegar
   Salt and freshly ground pepper

CROSTINI

1   small, slender baguette, cut on the diagonal into slices ¼ inch (6 mm) thick
   Extra-virgin olive oil for drizzling

In a colander, toss the diced eggplant with a generous amount of salt. Place the colander in a sink or over another bowl and let drain for 1 hour. Rinse the eggplant with cold running water to remove the salt and bitter juices, then pat dry with paper towels or roll up in a kitchen towel.

In a small frying pan over medium-high heat, pour in olive oil to a depth of ½ inch (12 mm). When hot but not smoking, add the eggplant in several batches; do not crowd the pan. Fry, stirring occasionally, until tender and golden brown, 6–8 minutes. Using a slotted spoon, transfer the eggplant to a double thickness of paper towels to drain. Fry the zucchini in the same pan in the same manner, adding more oil as needed to measure ½ inch (12 mm) deep; transfer the zucchini to paper towels to drain. In a nonaluminum bowl, combine the eggplant and zucchini and set aside.

In a frying pan over medium heat, warm the 2 tablespoons olive oil. Add the onion and celery and sauté until tender, 5–7 minutes. Add the tomato-basil sauce, olives, garlic and capers and cook, stirring occasionally, until the sauce thickens slightly, 5–8 minutes. Stir in ¼ cup (2 oz/60 g)

sugar and ¼ cup (2 fl oz/60 ml) vinegar and simmer, stirring constantly, until the sugar dissolves completely. Stir in salt and pepper to taste. Taste and add more sugar and vinegar as necessary to achieve a good sweet-sour balance. Add the sauce mixture to the eggplant and zucchini and toss together gently. Cover and refrigerate for at least 12 hours or for up to 3 days before serving.

When ready to serve, bring the eggplant mixture to room temperature. To make the crostini, preheat an oven to 400°F (200°C). Place the baguette slices in a large bowl and drizzle with a bit of olive oil. Toss the slices until the oil is evenly distributed (they should be slightly moistened, not coated). Lay the slices in a single layer on a large baking sheet. Bake, turning once, until lightly golden and crisp, 5–7 minutes. Watch carefully, as they burn easily.

Spoon the eggplant mixture onto individual plates or a platter and surround with the warm crostini.

Serves 10–12

White Beans in Tomato-Sage Sauce

In this traditional recipe from Tuscany, white beans are served all'uccelletto, *seasoned with tomato sauce scented with earthy sage. The secret to perfect white beans is to cook them at the barest simmer. The less they move around in the pot, the better they retain their shape.*

1½ cups (10 oz/315 g) dried cannellini or Great Northern beans
Salt

½ cup (4 fl oz/125 ml) extra-virgin olive oil, plus olive oil for serving

8 plum (Roma) tomatoes, peeled, seeded and coarsely chopped, or 1 can (16 oz/500 g) plum (Roma) tomatoes with their juices, coarsely chopped

8 large fresh sage leaves or 1 tablespoon dried sage, crumbled

2 cloves garlic, minced
Freshly ground pepper

Sort through the beans, discarding any misshapen beans or stones. Rinse the beans well by swishing them around in a large bowl with plenty of water. Drain and transfer to a large, heavy cooking pot, preferably of flameproof earthenware. Add water to cover by about 3 inches (7.5 cm) and bring to a rolling boil. Immediately reduce the heat to low so that the water is barely simmering, cover and cook until the beans are very soft yet still hold their shape, about 1¼ hours. As the beans cook, check the water level occasionally and add another cup or so of hot water if the level drops. When the beans are done, add salt to taste and remove from the heat. Leave the beans in their cooking liquid until ready to mix with the tomato sauce.

In a large frying pan over medium heat, warm the ½ cup (4 fl oz/ 125 ml) olive oil. Add the tomatoes and cook, stirring frequently, until they begin to break down and form a sauce, about 10 minutes. Add the sage and garlic and season to taste with salt and pepper. Continue cooking, stirring occasionally, until the sauce has thickened and most of the liquid has evaporated, about 10 minutes.

Drain the beans, reserving 1 cup (8 fl oz/250 ml) of the cooking liquid. Add the beans to the sauce and toss gently to mix. Add the reserved cooking liquid, 1 tablespoon at a time, as needed to moisten the dish. It should be thick and saucelike in consistency. Transfer to a serving dish and let cool until barely warm or to room temperature. Drizzle with a little olive oil before serving.

Serves 4–6

Tomato, Mozzarella and Basil Salad

With this colorful dish, the island of Capri, off Italy's southern coast, has given the world a fresh and delicate gift. Few ingredients are more perfectly suited than ripe summer tomatoes, fresh mozzarella and fragrant basil. Try to find the tiny balls of mozzarella called bocconcini, and Sweet 100s, a recent tomato variety of intensely sweet flavor.

¾ lb (375 g) fresh mozzarella cheese, drained

4 tablespoons (2 fl oz/60 ml) extra-virgin olive oil
Salt and freshly ground pepper

12 fresh basil leaves, thinly sliced

2 tablespoons coarsely chopped fresh flat-leaf (Italian) parsley

2 pints (12 oz/375 g) round and/or pear-shaped cherry tomatoes, in a mixture of colors

¼ cup (1½ oz/45 g) Moroccan olives or other oil-cured olives

◻ If using large balls of mozzarella, cut them into ½-inch (12-mm) dice. If using smaller balls, cut them into quarters.

◻ In a bowl, toss the mozzarella with 2 tablespoons of the olive oil and a generous sprinkling of salt and pepper. Add half of the basil and half of the parsley. Toss gently.

◻ If using round cherry tomatoes, cut them in half. If using pear-shaped tomatoes, leave them whole. In another bowl, combine the tomatoes with the remaining 2 tablespoons olive oil, salt and pepper to taste, and the remaining basil and parsley. Toss gently.

◻ Mound the mozzarella in the center of individual plates. Make a ring of the seasoned tomatoes around the edge and garnish with the olives. Serve immediately.

Serves 4–6

34

Grilled Eggplant and Goat Cheese Spirals

No antipasti selection would be complete without one or two eggplant dishes. Here, the eggplant is grilled, then marinated with herbs and combined with the mellow sharpness of fresh goat cheese.

1　eggplant (aubergine)
　　Salt
　　Olive oil for brushing
　　Freshly ground pepper
⅓　cup (½ oz/15 g) chopped fresh
　　chives
3　cloves garlic, minced
　　Balsamic vinegar for sprinkling
　　Leaves from 12 fresh thyme sprigs,
　　finely chopped, or 1 tablespoon
　　dried thyme, crumbled
1　log (7 oz/220 g) fresh goat cheese,
　　at room temperature

◎ Cut off and discard a thin slice from the stem and blossom ends of the eggplant. Cut the eggplant lengthwise into slices ¼ inch (6 mm) thick. Lay the slices on a double thickness of paper towels and sprinkle generously with salt. Let stand until beads of water appear on the surface, about 20 minutes. Rinse with cold running water to remove the salt and bitter juices, then pat dry with additional paper towels.

◎ Prepare a fire in a charcoal grill, or preheat a ridged stove-top griddle until it is very hot. Brush the eggplant slices lightly on one side with olive oil, then place them on the grill in a single layer, oiled sides down. Brush the tops with additional oil and grill until the eggplant begins to soften and the grill marks are clearly visible, then turn and continue grilling until soft but not too deeply browned, about 4 minutes total. As the eggplant slices are done, use tongs to transfer them to a large platter.

◎ Arrange half of the slices in a single layer on another platter and sprinkle with salt and pepper to taste. Scatter half each of the chives and garlic evenly over the slices and sprinkle with a little balsamic vinegar. Sprinkle all the thyme evenly over the top. Top with the remaining eggplant slices, again in a single layer, and scatter the remaining chives and garlic over the top. Sprinkle with a little more vinegar. Let stand in a cool place for at least 2 hours, or cover and refrigerate for up to 3 days.

◎ When ready to serve, carefully spread each eggplant slice with an equal amount of the goat cheese and roll up into a tight spiral. Secure with a toothpick, if desired. Serve at room temperature.

Serves 4–6

Pizzas and Calzone

The ancient Greeks, who occupied southern Italy for centuries, baked disks of risen bread dough in hot ovens to create edible plates soaked with drippings and seasonings from the main course. This practice led to topping the dough with seasonings before it went into the oven, yielding the oldest ancestor of the Neapolitan pizza. Some food scholars have reasoned that calzone—simply pizzas folded in half over their fillings before being baked—were first devised as neat edible food pouches to nourish hungry travelers.

Ingenious Neapolitans changed pizzas and calzone forever with the addition of the *pomodoro,* "tomato," a food that Italians once believed to be poisonous. This succulent fruit became the staple topping for most pizzas, a fact immortalized and given the royal seal of approval in 1889 with the pizza named for Queen Margherita.

This food that has traveled so widely and been embraced by so many cultures continues to evolve. As tastes change and ingredients from kitchens around the world become more widely available, contemporary pizzerias try different calzone fillings and pizza toppings, from chicken and spinach enveloped in a creamy béchamel sauce to smoked salmon paired with smoked mozzarella, and radicchio and shrimp spiced with caramelized garlic.

Pizza with Asparagus and Artichokes

It is common to see seasonal offerings in pizzerias throughout
Italy. Here, asparagus and artichokes celebrate the arrival of spring.

Ice water

3   baby artichokes, trimmed *(see glossary, page 124)* and halved lengthwise

Salt

10   asparagus tips, each about 2 inches (5 cm) long

3   thin slices yellow onion, optional

Olive oil, if using onion

4–6   caramelized garlic cloves *(see recipe method on page 55),* optional

½   recipe Neapolitan pizza dough *(recipe on page 12),* completed through the second rising

All-purpose (plain) flour for dusting

5   fresh basil leaves, torn into small pieces

3   oz (90 g) Fontina cheese, sliced

Freshly ground pepper

2   tablespoons freshly grated Italian Parmesan cheese

1   tablespoon coarsely chopped fresh flat-leaf (Italian) parsley

▦ Fill a saucepan three-fourths full with water. Have ready a bowl of ice water. Trim the stems of the artichoke halves even with the bottoms. Add the halves to the saucepan; add salt to taste and bring to a boil. Cook the artichokes until tender when pierced with a knife, about 10 minutes. Remove and immerse in the ice water to halt the cooking. Drain and lay on paper towels to dry.

▦ Ready a second bowl of ice water. Bring a sauté pan three-fourths full of lightly salted water to a boil. Add the asparagus tips and blanch for 6–8 seconds. Remove and immerse in the ice water to halt the cooking. Drain and lay on paper towels to dry.

▦ If using the onion slices, in a small frying pan over medium heat, warm enough olive oil to coat the bottom of the pan lightly. Add the onion and sauté until soft, 8–10 minutes. Remove from the heat and set aside. If using the caramelized garlic cloves, prepare as directed and set aside.

▦ Place a pizza stone or unglazed terra-cotta tiles on the lowest rack of an oven. Preheat to 500°F (260°C).

▦ Place the dough on a lightly floured pizza peel or rimless baking sheet. Sprinkle on a little more flour and press evenly into a disk about 1½ inches (4 cm) thick and 5 inches (13 cm) in diameter. Lift the dough and gently stretch it with your fingers and then over the backs of your fists, using the weight of the dough to allow it to grow in size. Stretch and rotate the dough until it is about ¼ inch (6 mm) thick and 9 inches (23 cm) in diameter and has a rim about ½ inch (12 mm) thick. Try not to let the center of the disk become too thin. Dust the peel or baking sheet with more flour and gently lay the disk in the center.

▦ Arrange the asparagus, artichoke hearts, and onion slices and garlic, if using, evenly atop the dough, then scatter the basil over all. Arrange the Fontina slices evenly over the vegetables, and season to taste with salt and pepper. Gently shake the peel or baking sheet to make sure the pizza has not stuck to it. Using the peel or baking sheet like a large spatula, quickly slide the pizza onto the hot pizza stone or tiles.

▦ Bake until the edges are golden and crisp, 8–9 minutes. Remove the pizza with a large metal spatula and slide it onto a dinner plate. Sprinkle the Parmesan and parsley evenly over the pizza and serve at once.

Makes one 9-inch (23-cm) pizza

Pizza with Tomatoes, Mozzarella and Basil

Legend relates that this delicious and patriotic combination was created for Queen Margherita of Italy in 1889 by Don Raffaele Esposito, owner of the era's most famous pizzeria in Naples. Its ingredients honored the colors of her country's flag—red, white and green.

½ recipe Neapolitan pizza dough *(recipe on page 12),* completed through the second rising

All-purpose (plain) flour for dusting

⅓ cup (3 fl oz/80 ml) tomato-basil sauce *(recipe on page 14)*

6 fresh basil leaves

¼ lb (125 g) mozzarella cheese, sliced

◉ Place a pizza stone or unglazed terra-cotta tiles on the lowest rack of an oven. Preheat to 500°F (260°C).

◉ Place the ball of dough on a lightly floured pizza peel or rimless baking sheet. Sprinkle a little more flour on the top of the dough and, using your fingertips, press evenly into a round, flat disk about 1½ inches (4 cm) thick and 5 inches (13 cm) in diameter. Lift the dough and gently stretch it with your fingers and then over the backs of your fists, using the weight of the dough to allow it to grow in size. While you are stretching the dough, gently rotate the disk. Continue stretching and rotating the dough until it is about ¼ inch (6 mm) thick and 9 inches (23 cm) in diameter and has a rim about ½ inch (12 mm) thick. Try not to let the center of the disk become too thin in comparison to the edges. Dust the peel or baking sheet with more flour and gently lay the disk in the center.

◉ Place the tomato-basil sauce in the center of the disk. Using the back of a spoon, gently spread the sauce over the dough, leaving a 1-inch (2.5-cm) border free of sauce. Lay the basil leaves atop the sauce and then arrange the mozzarella slices evenly over all.

◉ Gently shake the peel or baking sheet back and forth to make sure the pizza has not stuck to it. If it has, gently lift off the stuck section and sprinkle a little more flour underneath. Using the peel or baking sheet like a large spatula, quickly slide the pizza onto the hot pizza stone or tiles.

◉ Bake until the edges are golden and crisp, 8–9 minutes. Remove the pizza with a large metal spatula and slide it onto a dinner plate. Serve at once.

Makes one 9-inch (23-cm) pizza

Pizza with Onion, Anchovies and Olives

Cooks on both the Italian and French Rivieras, from Liguria up through Provence, often combine the sweetness of sautéed onions and full-flavored tomatoes with the sharp bite of anchovy and brine-cured olives. Some food historians contend that the famed savory Provençal tart, la pissaladière, *originally comes from the Italian pizza* all'Andrea, *named for the renowned naval officer, Andrea Doria.*

2 tablespoons extra-virgin olive oil, plus olive oil for drizzling

1 small yellow onion, thinly sliced

   Salt and freshly ground pepper

½ recipe Neapolitan pizza dough *(recipe on page 12),* completed through the second rising

   All-purpose (plain) flour for dusting

4–6 plum (Roma) tomatoes, cut into slices ¼ inch (6 mm) thick

5 anchovy fillets, rinsed and patted dry

10 Kalamata or other brine-cured black olives, pitted

½ teaspoon dried oregano, crumbled

▣ Place a pizza stone or unglazed terra-cotta tiles on the lowest rack of an oven. Preheat to 500°F (260°C).

▣ In a large, heavy sauté pan over medium heat, warm the 2 tablespoons olive oil. Add the onion and sauté, stirring occasionally, until completely wilted and golden, about 10 minutes. Season to taste with salt and pepper and remove from the heat.

▣ Place the ball of dough on a lightly floured pizza peel or rimless baking sheet. Sprinkle a little more flour on the top of the dough and, with your fingertips, press evenly into a round, flat disk about 1½ inches (4 cm) thick and 5 inches (13 cm) in diameter. Lift the dough and gently stretch it with your fingers and then over the backs of your fists, using the weight of the dough to allow it to grow in size. While you are stretching the dough, gently rotate the disk. Continue stretching and rotating the dough until it is about ¼ inch (6 mm) thick and 9 inches (23 cm) in diameter and has a rim about ½ inch (12 mm) thick. Try not to let the center of the disk become too thin in comparison to the edges. Dust the peel or baking sheet with more flour and gently lay the disk in the center.

▣ Scatter the onions evenly over the dough. Distribute the sliced tomatoes evenly over the onions. Tear the anchovies into little pieces and scatter them evenly over the tomatoes. Finally, top with the olives and the oregano. Season to taste with salt and pepper and drizzle with a little extra-virgin olive oil.

▣ Gently shake the peel or baking sheet back and forth to make sure the pizza has not stuck to it. If it has, gently lift off the stuck section and sprinkle a little more flour underneath. Using the peel or baking sheet like a large spatula, quickly slide the pizza onto the hot pizza stone or tiles.

▣ Bake until the edges are golden and crisp, 8–9 minutes. Remove the pizza with a large metal spatula and slide it onto a dinner plate. Drizzle with additional olive oil, if desired, and serve at once.

Makes one 9-inch (23-cm) pizza

Pizza with Scallops and Pesto

*At seaside pizzerias all over Italy, treasures from the sea find their way
atop the familiar disk of dough. In this recipe, the intense heat of the oven sears
the marinated sea scallops as they sit on a layer of emerald pesto.*

6   large, plump sea scallops, about
    5 oz (155 g) total weight, cut in
    half horizontally if very thick
1   tablespoon extra-virgin olive oil,
    plus olive oil for drizzling
    Juice of ½ lemon
1   tablespoon coarsely chopped
    fresh flat-leaf (Italian) parsley
2   green (spring) onions, including
    the pale green tops, thinly sliced
    Salt and coarsely ground pepper
½   recipe Neapolitan pizza dough
    (recipe on page 12), completed
    through the second rising
    All-purpose (plain) flour for
    dusting
1   clove garlic
1   tablespoon Genovese pesto
    (recipe on page 15)

▨ In a small bowl, combine the scallops, 1 tablespoon olive oil, lemon juice, parsley, green onions, and salt and pepper to taste. Stir to mix well, cover and let stand for 20 minutes.

▨ Meanwhile, place a pizza stone or unglazed terra-cotta tiles on the lowest rack of an oven. Preheat to 500°F (260°C).

▨ Place the ball of dough on a lightly floured pizza peel or rimless baking sheet. Sprinkle a little more flour on the top of the dough and, using your fingertips, press evenly into a round, flat disk about 1½ inches (4 cm) thick and 5 inches (13 cm) in diameter. Lift the dough and gently stretch it with your fingers and then over the backs of your fists, using the weight of the dough to allow it to grow in size. While you are stretching the dough, gently rotate the disk. Continue stretching and rotating the dough until it is about ¼ inch (6 mm) thick and 9 inches (23 cm) in diameter and has a rim about ½ inch (12 mm) thick. Try not to let the center of the disk become too thin in comparison to the edges. Dust the peel or baking sheet with more flour and gently lay the disk in the center.

▨ Pass the garlic clove through a press held over the dough, then rub the garlic evenly over the surface. Using the back of a tablespoon, spread the pesto as evenly as possible over the dough. Using a slotted spoon, remove the scallops from their marinade and distribute them over the dough. Sprinkle a little of the marinade over the top.

▨ Gently shake the peel or baking sheet back and forth to make sure the pizza has not stuck to it. If it has, gently lift off the stuck section and sprinkle a little more flour underneath. Using the peel or baking sheet like a large spatula, quickly slide the pizza onto the hot pizza stone or tiles.

▨ Bake until the edges are golden and crisp, 8–9 minutes. Remove the pizza with a large metal spatula and slide it onto a dinner plate. Drizzle with olive oil, if desired, and serve at once.

Makes one 9-inch (23-cm) pizza

Calzone with Chicken and Spinach

While not a traditional ingredient in Italian pizzerias, chicken has been embraced by pizza cooks outside of Italy. Here, a creamy filling of tender dark meat, spinach and prosciutto is tucked into a calzone for an especially rich treat.

1　chicken thigh
　　Salt and freshly ground pepper

BÉCHAMEL SAUCE
½　cup (4 fl oz/125 ml) milk
1　tablespoon unsalted butter
1　tablespoon all-purpose (plain) flour
　　Salt and freshly ground pepper

1　bunch spinach, stems removed
1　thin slice prosciutto, chopped
2　tablespoons freshly grated Italian Parmesan cheese
½　recipe Neapolitan pizza dough *(recipe on page 12),* completed through the second rising
　　All-purpose (plain) flour for dusting

▣ Preheat an oven to 400°F (200°C). Place the chicken thigh in a baking pan and season with salt and pepper. Roast until golden brown and the juices run clear when the meat is pricked with a knife, 25–30 minutes. Remove and discard the skin and bone and shred the meat.

▣ To make the béchamel sauce, heat the milk in a small saucepan over medium-low heat until small bubbles appear along the pan edge. In another small saucepan over medium-low heat, melt the butter. Add the flour and whisk to form a smooth paste. Reduce the heat to low and cook, stirring, for about 2 minutes. When the milk is hot, add the butter-flour mixture, whisking constantly until it comes to a simmer. Simmer over medium heat until the sauce thickens enough to coat a spoon, about 20 minutes. Season with salt and pepper. Pour into a cup.

▣ Rinse the spinach but do not dry. Place in a saucepan over medium-low heat, cover and cook, turning occasionally, until wilted, 2–4 minutes. Drain and squeeze to remove the liquid. Chop coarsely.

▣ Place a pizza stone or unglazed terra-cotta tiles on the lowest rack of an oven. Preheat to 500°F (260°C).

▣ In a bowl, combine the shredded chicken, spinach, béchamel, prosciutto and Parmesan. Stir to mix well.

▣ Place the dough on a lightly floured pizza peel or rimless baking sheet. Sprinkle more flour on top and press evenly into a round disk about 1½ inches (4 cm) thick and 5 inches (13 cm) in diameter. Lift the dough and stretch with your fingers and then over the backs of your fists while gently rotating the disk. Continue until the dough is about ¼ inch (6 mm) thick and 8 inches (20 cm) in diameter. Dust the peel or baking sheet with more flour and lay the disk in the center.

▣ Mound the filling in the center of the dough that is nearest to you and fold over the filling, stretching as necessary so the edges meet. Crimp the edges to seal. Tear a steam vent about 1 inch (2.5 cm) long in the center of the top.

▣ Using the peel or baking sheet like a large spatula, quickly slide the calzone onto the hot pizza stone or tiles. Bake until the top is golden brown, 8–9 minutes. Remove from the oven and serve.

Makes 1 calzone

Pizza with Smoked Salmon and Mozzarella

This inspired American combination of the sophisticated tastes of smoked salmon and smoked mozzarella found its way back to the high-tech elegance of some urban Italian pizzerias. A squeeze of fresh lemon and a sprinkling of Italian parsley brighten the assertive flavors.

½   recipe Neapolitan pizza dough *(recipe on page 12)*, completed through the second rising

All-purpose (plain) flour for dusting

2   oz (60 g) thinly sliced smoked salmon

¼   lb (125 g) smoked mozzarella cheese, sliced

1½   teaspoons chopped fresh chives

Freshly ground pepper

Extra-virgin olive oil for drizzling

Juice of ½ lemon

1   tablespoon coarsely chopped fresh flat-leaf (Italian) parsley

◫ Place a pizza stone or unglazed terra-cotta tiles on the lowest rack of an oven. Preheat to 500°F (260°C).

◫ Place the ball of dough on a lightly floured pizza peel or rimless baking sheet. Sprinkle a little more flour on the top of the dough and, using your fingertips, press evenly into a round, flat disk about 1½ inches (4 cm) thick and 5 inches (13 cm) in diameter. Lift the dough and gently stretch it with your fingers and then over the backs of your fists, using the weight of the dough to allow it to grow in size. While you are stretching the dough, gently rotate the disk. Continue stretching and rotating the dough until it is about ¼ inch (6 mm) thick and 9 inches (23 cm) in diameter and has a rim about ½ inch (12 mm) thick. Try not to let the center of the disk become too thin in comparison to the edges. Dust the peel or baking sheet with more flour and gently lay the disk in the center.

◫ Arrange the smoked salmon on the dough. Top evenly with the smoked mozzarella slices and sprinkle with the chives. Season to taste with pepper. Finish with a drizzle of olive oil.

◫ Gently shake the peel or baking sheet back and forth to make sure the pizza has not stuck to it. If it has, gently lift off the stuck section and sprinkle a little more flour underneath. Using the peel or baking sheet like a large spatula, quickly slide the pizza onto the hot pizza stone or tiles.

◫ Bake until the edges are golden and crisp, 8–9 minutes. Remove the pizza with a large metal spatula and slide it onto a dinner plate. Sprinkle the lemon juice and parsley evenly over the top. Drizzle with additional olive oil, if desired, and serve at once.

Makes one 9-inch (23-cm) pizza

Pizza with Yellow Pepper and Capers

This pizza recalls late-night summer meals taken on the large outdoor terraces of country pizzerias in Italy's fabled south. Sweet yellow peppers are combined with mozzarella, capers and tomatoes for an exceptionally pretty pie. An amber beer, icy from the cooler, is the ideal accompaniment.

½ recipe Neapolitan pizza dough *(recipe on page 12),* completed through the second rising
  All-purpose (plain) flour for dusting

¼ lb (125 g) mozzarella cheese, sliced

1 ripe plum (Roma) tomato, cut in half lengthwise and then into slices ¼ inch (6 mm) thick

½ large, meaty yellow bell pepper (capsicum), seeded, deribbed and cut lengthwise into narrow strips

1 teaspoon capers, rinsed and drained
  Salt and freshly ground pepper
  Extra-virgin olive oil for drizzling

1 tablespoon coarsely chopped fresh flat-leaf (Italian) parsley

▣ Place a pizza stone or unglazed terra-cotta tiles on the lowest rack of an oven. Preheat to 500°F (260°C).

▣ Place the ball of dough on a lightly floured pizza peel or rimless baking sheet. Sprinkle a little more flour on the top of the dough and, using your fingertips, press evenly into a round, flat disk about 1½ inches (4 cm) thick and 5 inches (13 cm) in diameter. Lift the dough and gently stretch it with your fingers and then over the backs of your fists, using the weight of the dough to allow it to grow in size. While you are stretching the dough, gently rotate the disk. Continue stretching and rotating the dough until it is about ¼ inch (6 mm) thick and 9 inches (23 cm) in diameter and has a rim about ½ inch (12 mm) thick. Try not to let the center of the disk become too thin in comparison to the edges. Dust the peel or baking sheet with more flour and gently lay the disk in the center.

▣ Arrange the mozzarella evenly on the pizza dough. Top with the tomato slices, pepper strips and capers. Season to taste with salt and pepper and drizzle with a little olive oil.

▣ Gently shake the peel or baking sheet back and forth to make sure the pizza has not stuck to it. If it has, gently lift off the stuck section and sprinkle a little more flour underneath. Using the peel or baking sheet like a large spatula, quickly slide the pizza onto the hot pizza stone or tiles.

▣ Bake until the edges are golden and crisp, 8–9 minutes. Remove the pizza with a large metal spatula and slide it onto a dinner plate. Sprinkle with the parsley, drizzle with additional olive oil, if desired, and serve at once.

Makes one 9-inch (23-cm) pizza

Pizza with Radicchio and Fontina

A study in muted colors and complex flavors, this pizza from Treviso
in northern Italy combines two popular regional ingredients, radicchio and Fontina
cheese. Tender, pink shrimp are added to enrich the savory dish.

CARAMELIZED GARLIC

6   cloves garlic
     Olive oil, to cover

6   large shrimp (prawns), peeled,
     deveined and halved lengthwise

1   tablespoon extra-virgin olive oil,
     plus olive oil for drizzling
     Salt and coarsely ground pepper

½   recipe Neapolitan pizza dough
     (recipe on page 12), completed
     through the second rising

¼   head radicchio (red chicory),
     core removed and coarsely
     chopped

1½   tablespoons finely shredded
     fresh basil

4–5 oz (125–155 g) Fontina cheese,
     sliced

▣ To make the caramelized garlic, peel the garlic but leave the cloves whole. In a small, heavy saucepan over medium-low heat, combine the garlic cloves with just enough olive oil to cover. Bring to a gentle simmer and cook the garlic until it is covered with golden dots, about 15 minutes. Watch carefully, as the garlic burns easily. Remove from the heat, let cool and then drain off the oil. Set the garlic aside. Reserve the oil for another use such as drizzling over grilled fish or vegetables.

▣ Place a pizza stone or unglazed terra-cotta tiles on the lowest rack of an oven. Preheat to 500°F (260°C).

▣ In a small bowl, mix together the shrimp, 1 tablespoon extra-virgin olive oil, and salt and pepper to taste.

▣ Place the ball of dough on a lightly floured pizza peel or rimless baking sheet. Sprinkle a little more flour on the top of the dough and, using your fingertips, press evenly into a round, flat disk about 1½ inches (4 cm) thick and 5 inches (13 cm) in diameter. Lift the dough and gently stretch it with your fingers and then over the backs of your fists, using the weight of the dough to allow it to grow in size. While you are stretching the dough, gently rotate the disk.

Continue stretching and rotating the dough until it is about ¼ inch (6 mm) thick and 9 inches (23 cm) in diameter and has a rim about ½ inch (12 mm) thick. Try not to let the center of the disk become too thin in comparison to the edges. Dust the peel or baking sheet with more flour and gently lay the disk in the center.

▣ Scatter the radicchio, garlic and basil over the dough. Top evenly with the cheese and, finally, with the shrimp. Season to taste with salt and pepper and drizzle with a little extra-virgin olive oil.

▣ Gently shake the peel or baking sheet back and forth to make sure the pizza has not stuck to it. If it has, gently lift off the stuck section and sprinkle a little more flour underneath. Using the peel or baking sheet like a large spatula, quickly slide the pizza onto the hot pizza stone or tiles.

▣ Bake until the edges are golden and crisp, 8–9 minutes. Remove the pizza with a large metal spatula and slide it onto a dinner plate. Drizzle with additional extra-virgin olive oil, if desired, and serve at once.

Makes one 9-inch (23-cm) pizza

Pizza with Sausage and Mushrooms

The simple combination of sausage and mushrooms is often elevated by the use of chicken or duck sausage and shiitake or portobello mushrooms.

1   chicken or duck sausage, about ¼ lb (125 g), casing removed and meat crumbled

2   tablespoons extra-virgin olive oil, plus olive oil for drizzling

1   small yellow onion, thinly sliced

1   cup (3 oz/90 g) sliced, stemmed fresh shiitake or portobello mushrooms

1   clove garlic, minced

1   teaspoon minced fresh thyme
    Salt and freshly ground pepper

½   recipe Neapolitan pizza dough *(recipe on page 12)*, completed through the second rising
    All-purpose (plain) flour for dusting

¼   lb (125 g) mozzarella or Fontina cheese, sliced

2   tablespoons freshly grated Italian Parmesan cheese

◻ Place the crumbled sausage in a small sauté pan or frying pan over medium heat and sauté, stirring often, until crumbly and cooked through, 10–15 minutes. Remove from the heat and set aside.

◻ In a large, heavy sauté pan over medium heat, warm the 2 tablespoons olive oil. Add the onion and sauté, stirring frequently, until completely wilted, about 10 minutes. Add the mushrooms, garlic and thyme and continue cooking over medium heat until the onions are golden and the mushrooms are tender, about 5 minutes longer. Season to taste with salt and pepper and remove from the heat.

◻ Place a pizza stone or unglazed terra-cotta tiles on the lowest rack of an oven. Preheat to 500°F (260°C).

◻ Place the ball of dough on a lightly floured pizza peel or rimless baking sheet. Sprinkle a little more flour on the top of the dough and, using your fingertips, press evenly into a round, flat disk about 1½ inches (4 cm) thick and 5 inches (13 cm) in diameter. Lift the dough and gently stretch it with your fingers and then over the backs of your fists, using the weight of the dough to allow it to grow in size. While you are stretching the dough, gently rotate the disk.

Continue stretching and rotating the dough until it is about ¼ inch (6 mm) thick and 9 inches (23 cm) in diameter and has a rim about ½ inch (12 mm) thick. Try not to let the center of the disk become too thin in comparison to the edges. Dust the peel or baking sheet with more flour and gently lay the disk in the center.

◻ Spread the onion-shiitake mixture evenly over the dough, then scatter on the sausage. Top evenly with the cheese slices.

◻ Gently shake the peel or baking sheet back and forth to make sure the pizza has not stuck to it. If it has, gently lift off the stuck section and sprinkle a little more flour underneath. Using the peel or baking sheet like a large spatula, quickly slide the pizza onto the hot pizza stone or tiles.

◻ Bake until the edges are golden and crisp, 8–9 minutes. Remove the pizza with a large metal spatula and slide it onto a dinner plate. Sprinkle evenly with the Parmesan and serve at once.

Makes one 9-inch (23-cm) pizza

Calzone with Assorted Meats and Cheeses

Walk into any salumeria—Italian delicatessen—and the aroma of countless cheeses and cured meats captivates the senses. The pungent flavors of salami, prosciutto and mortadella are mellowed by sweet ricotta and Parmesan cheese in this salute to the tradition of the salumeria.

2 tablespoons extra-virgin olive oil

1 small yellow onion, thinly sliced
Salt and freshly ground pepper

½ cup (4 oz/125 g) ricotta cheese

2 thin slices salami, coarsely chopped

1 slice prosciutto, coarsely chopped

1 slice mortadella, coarsely chopped

½ recipe Neapolitan pizza dough *(recipe on page 12)*, completed through the second rising
All-purpose (plain) flour for dusting

¼ cup (2 fl oz/60 ml) tomato-basil sauce *(recipe on page 14)*

1 tablespoon freshly grated Italian Parmesan cheese

◈ Place a pizza stone or unglazed terra-cotta tiles on the lowest rack of an oven. Preheat to 500°F (260°C).

◈ In a large, heavy sauté pan over medium heat, warm the olive oil. Add the onion and sauté until completely wilted and golden, about 10 minutes. Season to taste with salt and pepper and remove from the heat.

◈ In a bowl, combine the onion, ricotta, salami, prosciutto, mortadella and pepper to taste. Stir to mix well.

◈ Place the ball of dough on a lightly floured pizza peel or rimless baking sheet. Sprinkle a little more flour on the top of the dough and, using your fingertips, press evenly into a round, flat disk about 1½ inches (4 cm) thick and 5 inches (13 cm) in diameter. Lift the dough and gently stretch it with your fingers and then over the backs of your fists, using the weight of the dough to allow it to grow in size. While you are stretching the dough, gently rotate the disk. Continue stretching and rotating the dough until it is about ¼ inch (6 mm) thick and 8 inches (20 cm) in diameter. Try not to let the center of the disk become too thin in comparison to the edges. Dust the peel or baking sheet with more flour and gently lay the disk in the center.

◈ Mound the filling in the center on the half of the dough that is nearest to you. Gently fold the top half of the dough over the filling, stretching and adjusting as necessary so the edges meet. Crimp the edges with a fork to seal. Tear a steam vent about 1 inch (2.5 cm) long in the center of the top. Spoon the tomato-basil sauce over the vent and spread it around with the back of a spoon for decoration.

◈ Gently shake the peel or baking sheet back and forth to make sure the calzone has not stuck to it. If it has, gently lift off the stuck section and sprinkle a little more flour underneath. Using the peel or baking sheet like a large spatula, quickly slide the calzone onto the hot pizza stone or tiles. Bake until the top is golden brown and the bottom is dotted with dark brown spots, 8–9 minutes. Remove the calzone with a large metal spatula and place on a dinner plate. Sprinkle the Parmesan cheese over the top and serve at once.

Makes 1 calzone

Pizza with Goat Cheese and Zucchini

Imagine a pastore, or "shepherd," topping a thick piece of bread with his own freshly made goat cheese, a bit of zucchini and a scattering of leeks. This pizza is an homage to such pastoral combinations.

2 tablespoons extra-virgin olive oil, plus olive oil for drizzling

1 small zucchini (courgette), trimmed and cut into thin julienne strips

1 leek, white part only, carefully rinsed and thinly sliced crosswise

1 clove garlic, minced
   Salt and coarsely ground pepper

½ recipe Neapolitan pizza dough *(recipe on page 12),* completed through the second rising
   All-purpose (plain) flour for dusting

¼ lb (125 g) fresh goat cheese

1 teaspoon dried oregano, crumbled
   Juice of ½ lemon

▨ Place a pizza stone or unglazed terra-cotta tiles on the lowest rack of an oven. Preheat to 500°F (260°C).

▨ In a large sauté pan over medium heat, warm the 2 tablespoons olive oil. Add the zucchini, leek and garlic and sauté, stirring occasionally, until the vegetables are barely tender, 3–4 minutes. Season to taste with salt and pepper and remove from the heat. Set aside.

▨ Place the ball of dough on a lightly floured pizza peel or rimless baking sheet. Sprinkle a little more flour on the top of the dough and, using your fingertips, press evenly into a round, flat disk about 1½ inches (4 cm) thick and 5 inches (13 cm) in diameter. Lift the dough and gently stretch it with your fingers and then over the backs of your fists, using the weight of the dough to allow it to grow in size. While you are stretching the dough, gently rotate the disk. Continue stretching and rotating the dough until it is about ¼ inch (6 mm) thick and 9 inches (23 cm) in diameter and has a rim about ½ inch (12 mm) thick. Try not to let the center

of the disk become too thin in comparison to the edges. Dust the peel or baking sheet with more flour and gently lay the disk in the center.

▨ Distribute the zucchini-leek mixture evenly over the dough. Dot the pizza with the goat cheese and sprinkle with the oregano.

▨ Gently shake the peel or baking sheet back and forth to make sure the pizza has not stuck to it. If it has, gently lift off the stuck section and sprinkle a little more flour underneath. Using the peel or baking sheet like a large spatula, quickly slide the pizza onto the hot pizza stone or tiles.

▨ Bake until the edges are golden and crisp, 8–9 minutes. Remove the pizza with a large metal spatula and slide it onto a dinner plate. Sprinkle with the lemon juice and serve at once.

Makes one 9-inch (23-cm) pizza

Calzone with Eggplant, Pancetta and Mozzarella

Easily grown by nearly anyone with a bit of sun and a patch of earth, eggplant and tomatoes have long been staples of southern Italian cooking. Pancetta, unsmoked Italian bacon that is simply cured with salt and pepper, and slices of mozzarella add a rich touch to this savory calzone.

¼ cup (2 fl oz/60 ml) extra-virgin olive oil

2 tablespoons coarsely chopped pancetta or thick-cut bacon

2 Asian (slender) eggplants (aubergines), ends trimmed, peeled and diced

Salt and coarsely ground pepper

½ recipe Neapolitan pizza dough *(recipe on page 12),* completed through the second rising

All-purpose (plain) flour for dusting

1½ teaspoons finely shredded fresh basil

3 oz (90 g) mozzarella cheese, sliced

⅓ cup (3 fl oz/80 ml) tomato-basil sauce *(recipe on page 14)*

◼ Place a pizza stone or unglazed terra-cotta tiles on the lowest rack of an oven. Preheat to 500°F (260°C).

◼ In a large sauté pan over medium-low heat, warm the olive oil. Add the pancetta or bacon and sauté, stirring occasionally, until it renders its fat, about 5 minutes. Add the eggplants and increase the heat to medium. Sauté until the eggplants are golden brown and tender, 4–5 minutes. Season to taste with salt and pepper and remove from the heat.

◼ Place the ball of dough on a lightly floured pizza peel or rimless baking sheet. Sprinkle a little more flour on the top of the dough and, using your fingertips, press evenly into a round, flat disk about 1½ inches (4 cm) thick and 5 inches (13 cm) in diameter. Lift the dough and gently stretch it with your fingers and then over the backs of your fists, using the weight of the dough to allow it to grow in size. While you are stretching the dough, gently rotate the disk. Continue stretching and rotating the dough until it is about ¼ inch (6 mm) thick and 8 inches (20 cm) in diameter. Try not to let the center of the disk become too thin in comparison

to the edges. Dust the peel or baking sheet with more flour and gently lay the disk in the center.

◼ Mound the eggplant mixture in the center on the half of the dough that is nearest to you. Top with the basil, mozzarella and tomato-basil sauce. Gently fold the top half of the dough over the filling, stretching and adjusting as necessary so the edges meet. Crimp the edges with a fork to seal. Tear a steam vent about 1 inch (2.5 cm) long in the center of the top.

◼ Gently shake the peel or baking sheet back and forth to make sure the calzone has not stuck to it. If it has, gently lift off the stuck section and sprinkle a little more flour underneath. Using the peel or baking sheet like a large spatula, quickly slide the calzone onto the hot pizza stone or tiles.

◼ Bake until the top is golden brown and the bottom is dotted with dark brown spots. Remove the calzone with a large metal spatula and place on a dinner plate. Serve at once.

Makes 1 calzone

Pizza with Escarole and Pine Nuts

This traditional pairing of tender escarole with anchovies, pine nuts and bread crumbs is found on the tables of the more rustic pizzerias of Italy and in their more sophisticated Italian counterparts in America and elsewhere.

½ cup (4 fl oz/125 ml) water

2 tablespoons extra-virgin olive oil, plus olive oil for drizzling

½ head escarole (Batavian endive), tough outer leaves and core removed, coarsely chopped

1 clove garlic, minced

½ recipe Neapolitan pizza dough *(recipe on page 12),* completed through the second rising
All-purpose (plain) flour for dusting

¼ lb (125 g) Fontina cheese, sliced

2 anchovy fillets, rinsed, patted dry and chopped

1 tablespoon pine nuts
Freshly ground pepper

1 tablespoon toasted fine dried bread crumbs

▣ In a large sauté pan over medium-low heat, combine the water and the 2 tablespoons olive oil. Bring the liquid to a simmer and add the escarole and garlic. Cover and simmer until the escarole is tender, about 7 minutes. Transfer it to a colander to drain. When cool enough to handle, squeeze between the palms of your hands to remove as much liquid as possible.

▣ Place a pizza stone or unglazed terra-cotta tiles on the lowest rack of an oven. Preheat to 500°F (260°C).

▣ Place the ball of dough on a lightly floured pizza peel or rimless baking sheet. Sprinkle a little more flour on the top of the dough and, using your fingertips, press evenly into a round, flat disk about 1½ inches (4 cm) thick and 5 inches (13 cm) in diameter. Lift the dough and gently stretch it with your fingers and then over the backs of your fists, using the weight of the dough to allow it to grow in size. While you are stretching the dough, gently rotate the disk. Continue stretching and rotating the dough until it is about ¼ inch (6 mm) thick and 9 inches (23 cm) in diameter and has a rim about ½ inch (12 mm) thick. Try not to let the center of the disk become too thin in comparison to the edges. Dust the peel or baking sheet with more flour and gently lay the disk in the center.

▣ Arrange the escarole over the dough. Top evenly with the Fontina, then scatter on the anchovies and pine nuts. Season to taste with pepper. Finish with a drizzle of olive oil.

▣ Gently shake the peel or baking sheet back and forth to make sure the pizza has not stuck to it. If it has, gently lift off the stuck section and sprinkle a little more flour underneath. Using the peel or baking sheet like a large spatula, quickly slide the pizza onto the hot pizza stone or tiles.

▣ Bake until the edges are golden and crisp, 8–9 minutes. Remove the pizza with a large metal spatula and slide it onto a dinner plate. Scatter the bread crumbs evenly over the top and serve at once.

Makes one 9-inch (23-cm) pizza

Pizza with Spinach, Sausage, Salami and Red Pepper

This pizza is made in true American style—with more than half a dozen ingredients. Fennel-scented sweet Italian sausages combine well with the other toppings, but choose the type of sausage you prefer.

1   red bell pepper (capsicum)
1   sweet Italian sausage, about ¼ lb (125 g), casing removed and meat crumbled
½   bunch spinach, stems removed
    Salt
½   recipe Neapolitan pizza dough *(recipe on page 12),* completed through the second rising
    All-purpose (plain) flour for dusting
⅓   cup (3 fl oz/80 ml) uncooked tomato sauce *(recipe on page 14)*
2   paper-thin slices yellow onion, each cut in half
4   thin slices salami, torn into pieces
1   thin slice prosciutto, coarsely chopped
¼   lb (125 g) mozzarella cheese, sliced
2   tablespoons freshly grated Italian Parmesan cheese

▣ Preheat a broiler (griller) or preheat an oven to 450°F (230°C). Set the pepper on a baking sheet and place in the broiler or oven. Broil (grill) or bake, turning as necessary, until the skin is charred on all sides. Immediately place in a bowl and cover tightly. Let steam until cool, about 15 minutes. Peel off the charred skin, then pull out and discard the stems and seeds. Cut in half lengthwise and trim away any tough white ribs. Cut into long, narrow strips.

▣ Place a pizza stone or unglazed terra-cotta tiles on the lowest rack of an oven. Preheat to 500°F (260°C).

▣ Place the sausage in a small frying pan over medium heat. Sauté, stirring often, until crumbly and cooked through, 10–15 minutes.

▣ Meanwhile, rinse the spinach but do not dry. Place in a saucepan over medium-low heat, sprinkle with salt, cover and cook, turning occasionally, until wilted, 2–4 minutes. Drain and squeeze to remove the liquid. Chop coarsely.

▣ Place the dough on a lightly floured pizza peel or rimless baking sheet. Sprinkle more flour on top and press evenly into a round disk about 1½ inches (4 cm) thick and 5 inches (13 cm) in diameter. Lift the dough and stretch with your fingers and then over the backs of your fists, while gently rotating the disk. Continue until the dough is ¼ inch (6 mm) thick and 9 inches (23 cm) in diameter and has a rim ½ inch (12 mm) thick. Dust the peel or baking sheet with more flour and lay the disk in the center.

▣ Place the tomato sauce in the center of the disk. Using the back of a spoon, gently spread the sauce over the dough, leaving a 1-inch (2.5-cm) border free of sauce. Scatter the cooked sausage over the sauce, then layer on the spinach, bell pepper, onion, salami and prosciutto. Top evenly with the mozzarella and dust with the Parmesan.

▣ Gently shake the peel or baking sheet back and forth to make sure the pizza has not stuck to it. If it has, lift off the stuck section and sprinkle more flour underneath. Using the peel or baking sheet like a large spatula, quickly slide the pizza onto the hot pizza stone or tiles.

▣ Bake until the edges are golden and crisp, 8–9 minutes. Remove and slide onto a dinner plate. Serve at once.

Makes one 9-inch (23-cm) pizza

Pizza with Sun-Dried Tomatoes

Pumate are the famous sun-dried tomatoes of Apulia, the region tucked into the heel of the Italian boot. Driving along the country roads there, one sees flashes of scarlet on the outsides of many houses. They are plump bunches of Principessa Borghese tomatoes, a variety grown in summer and strung up to dry in the sun throughout the year. Packed in olive oil, they add an intensely sweet tomato flavor to any pizza.

¾ cup (1 oz/30 g) coarsely chopped arugula (rocket)

1 tablespoon extra-virgin olive oil
Salt and coarsely ground pepper

½ recipe Neapolitan pizza dough *(recipe on page 12),* completed through the second rising
All-purpose (plain) flour for dusting

1 clove garlic

2 fresh plum (Roma) tomatoes, cut into small dice

¼ cup (2 oz/60 g) drained oil-packed sun-dried tomatoes, coarsely chopped and oil reserved

¼ lb (125 g) mozzarella cheese, sliced

2 tablespoons freshly grated Italian Parmesan cheese

▣ Place a pizza stone or unglazed terra-cotta tiles on the lowest rack of an oven. Preheat to 500°F (260°C).

▣ In a small bowl, stir together the arugula, olive oil, and salt and pepper to taste.

▣ Place the ball of dough on a lightly floured pizza peel or rimless baking sheet. Sprinkle a little more flour on the top of the dough and, using your fingertips, press evenly into a round, flat disk about 1½ inches (4 cm) thick and 5 inches (13 cm) in diameter. Lift the dough and gently stretch it with your fingers and then over the backs of your fists, using the weight of the dough to allow it to grow in size. While you are stretching the dough, gently rotate the disk. Continue stretching and rotating the dough until it is about ¼ inch (6 mm) thick and 9 inches (23 cm) in diameter and has a rim about ½ inch (12 mm) thick. Try not to let the center of the disk become too thin in comparison to the edges. Dust the peel or baking sheet with more flour and gently lay the disk in the center.

▣ Pass the garlic clove through a press held over the dough, then rub the garlic evenly over the surface. Top with the fresh and sun-dried tomatoes. Spread the seasoned arugula over the tomatoes and distribute the mozzarella over the top.

▣ Gently shake the peel or baking sheet back and forth to make sure the pizza has not stuck to it. If it has, gently lift off the stuck section and sprinkle a little more flour underneath. Using the peel or baking sheet like a large spatula, quickly slide the pizza onto the hot pizza stone or tiles.

▣ Bake until the edges are golden and crisp, 8–9 minutes. Remove the pizza with a large metal spatula and slide it onto a dinner plate. Sprinkle evenly with the Parmesan, drizzle with the oil reserved from the tomatoes and serve at once.

Makes one 9-inch (23-cm) pizza

Focaccia and Panini

Centuries ago in northern Italy, the Etruscans baked *puls,* a thick gruel, under hot ashes, then topped the resultant cakes with oil and herbs, to eat with broth or meat. The Romans dubbed such rustic flat bread *panus focus,* "bread from the hearth," a name that later evolved into *focaccia.*

Focaccia is made from a softer, more yeasty dough than pizza and, unlike pizza, is usually served warm or at room temperature. Seasoned with herbs and sprinkled sparingly with coarse salt, sharp cheese or other piquant condiments, focaccia makes a satisfying accompaniment to a meal. It also becomes the perfect *merenda,* or "snack," on its own or the base for such hearty ingredients as sliced potatoes, pesto sauce and pine nuts.

Focaccia is a natural choice for constructing *panini,* the little sandwiches of Italy. Its rustic charm and appealing texture inspire many contemporary filling combinations, from a vegetarian ensemble of sautéed eggplant, tomatoes, mozzarella and basil to a distinctive combination of halibut, arugula and roasted peppers. However you bake it and top or fill it, focaccia finds a warm welcome on any pizzeria menu.

Focaccia with Red Onion

This focaccia is found on the menus of pizzerias in Florence, where small, three-wheel flatbed trucks laden with torpedo-shaped purple onions—their tops flopping over the edge of the bed—zoom into the city on market days.

½ recipe herb-flavored focaccia dough *(recipe on page 13)*, completed through the first rising

¼ small red (Spanish) onion, thinly sliced

1½ teaspoons chopped fresh thyme
Extra-virgin olive oil for drizzling

2–3 tablespoons freshly grated Italian Parmesan cheese

▨ Lightly oil an 8-inch (20-cm) cake pan or similar pan. Place the dough in the prepared pan and gently stretch it to the edges, pulling it from the center outward to achieve an even thickness. If the dough springs back toward the center and is difficult to work with, cover and set it aside to relax for 10 minutes, then continue coaxing the dough out to an even thickness. Cover with a kitchen towel and let rise until almost doubled in bulk and very soft and puffy, about 45 minutes.

▨ Preheat an oven to 475°F (245°C).

▨ Using your fingertips, dimple the dough vigorously in several places, leaving indentations about ½ inch (12 mm) deep. Again cover the pan with a towel and let rise for 20 minutes longer.

▨ Arrange the onion and thyme evenly over the risen dough. Drizzle the top with olive oil, then sprinkle on the Parmesan. Bake until golden brown and cooked through, 15–18 minutes. Transfer the pan to a rack and let stand until the focaccia is barely warm, about 10 minutes, then serve.

Makes one 8-inch (20-cm) focaccia round

Focaccia with Pesto and Potatoes

Potatoes and bread have a satisfying affinity for each other. A garlicky pesto sauce adds a luscious spark to this focaccia, perfect for lunch paired with a salad of baby greens. Although covered with potato slices, the pesto bubbles up during baking to contribute its special beauty to the finished round.

½   recipe herb-flavored focaccia dough *(recipe on page 13)*, completed through the first rising

2   tablespoons olive oil

½   small yellow onion, thinly sliced

2–3   tablespoons Genovese pesto *(recipe on page 15)*

1   very small russet or golden-fleshed potato, unpeeled, sliced paper-thin

2   tablespoons pine nuts

2   tablespoons freshly grated Italian Parmesan cheese

▨ Lightly oil an 8-inch (20-cm) cake pan or similar pan. Place the dough in the prepared pan and gently stretch it to the edges, pulling it from the center outward to achieve an even thickness. If the dough springs back toward the center and is difficult to work with, cover and set it aside to relax for 10 minutes, then continue coaxing the dough out to an even thickness. Cover with a kitchen towel and let rise until almost doubled in bulk and very soft and puffy, about 45 minutes.

▨ Preheat an oven to 475°F (245°C).

▨ Using your fingertips, dimple the dough vigorously in several places, leaving indentations about ½ inch (12 mm) deep. Again cover the pan with a towel and let rise for 20 minutes longer.

▨ While the dough is rising, in a small sauté pan over medium-low heat, warm the olive oil. Add the onion and sauté until tender and golden, about 6 minutes. Remove from the heat and let cool.

▨ Using the back of a spoon, spread the pesto evenly over the dough, using the larger amount if you want the finished focaccia to have a fuller pesto flavor. Arrange the potato slices in concentric circles atop the pesto, leaving gaps between the circles. Top evenly with the sautéed onion and the pine nuts. Scatter the Parmesan over the surface, including around the rim. Bake until golden brown and cooked through, 15–18 minutes. Transfer the pan to a rack and let stand until the focaccia is barely warm, about 10 minutes, then serve.

Makes one 8-inch (20-cm) focaccia round

Eggplant, Tomato and Mozzarella Sandwich

Here, the traditional ingredients for eggplant parmigiana are used to make a luscious panino. For a lighter version, grill rather than sauté the eggplant. The sandwich is delicious made while the eggplant is still warm. You can also marinate the sautéed eggplant with a bit of minced garlic, a few chopped basil leaves and a splash of balsamic vinegar, allowing you to assemble the panino another day.

1	Asian (slender) eggplant (aubergine)
2	tablespoons olive oil
	Focaccia with coarse salt *(recipe on page 80)* or focaccia with red onion *(page 72)*
1	tomato, sliced
2	thin slices Vidalia onion or other sweet onion
3	oz (90 g) fresh mozzarella cheese, sliced
3 or 4	fresh basil leaves
	Salt and freshly ground pepper
	Extra-virgin olive oil for drizzling
2	tablespoons freshly grated Italian Parmesan cheese

◈ Trim the ends from the eggplant and thinly slice crosswise. Discard the end slices that are covered on one side with skin. In a sauté pan over medium heat, warm the olive oil. Add the eggplant and cook, turning once, until tender and golden, 5–7 minutes. Using a slotted spoon, transfer to paper towels to drain.

◈ Slice the focaccia in half horizontally. Lay the bottom half, cut side up, on a cutting board. Arrange the eggplant slices on the bottom half.

Top evenly with the tomato, onion and mozzarella slices and the basil leaves. Season to taste with salt and pepper. Drizzle with olive oil and sprinkle the Parmesan evenly over the top. Place the other half of the focaccia on top, cut side down, and press down firmly with the palm of your hand. Cut the *panino* in half or in quarters for easier eating and serve.

Makes 1 sandwich

Focaccia with Cheese

Taleggio is a soft, creamy Italian cheese with a hint of acidic tang. It melts beautifully atop this savory focaccia. For the Taleggio, you may substitute a good-quality Jack cheese or Fontina.

½ recipe herb-flavored focaccia dough *(recipe on page 13)*, completed through the first rising

2 oz (60 g) Taleggio cheese, coarsely chopped

10 fresh sage leaves
    Salt and freshly ground pepper
    Extra-virgin olive oil for drizzling

◈ Lightly oil an 8-inch (20-cm) cake pan or similar pan. Place the dough in the prepared pan and gently stretch it to the edges, pulling it from the center outward to achieve an even thickness. If the dough springs back toward the center and is difficult to work with, cover and set it aside to relax for 10 minutes, then continue coaxing the dough out to an even thickness. Cover with a kitchen towel and let rise until almost doubled in bulk and very soft and puffy, about 45 minutes.

◈ Preheat an oven to 475°F (245°C).

◈ Using your fingertips, dimple the dough vigorously in several places, leaving indentations about ½ inch (12 mm) deep. Again cover the pan with a towel and let rise for 20 minutes longer.

◈ Top the risen dough evenly with the Taleggio cheese, sage and salt and pepper to taste. Drizzle the top with olive oil, making sure to coat the sage leaves evenly. Bake until golden brown and cooked through, 15–18 minutes. Transfer the pan to a rack and let stand until the focaccia is barely warm, about 10 minutes, then serve.

Makes one 8-inch (20-cm) focaccia round

Focaccia with Coarse Salt

In pizzerias, this simple focaccia is sometimes served with a tumbler of red wine before dinner. It can also be split in half and used to house a variety of fillings for panini.

½ recipe herb-flavored focaccia dough *(recipe on page 13)*, completed through the first rising

1½ teaspoons coarse salt
Coarsely ground pepper

1½ tablespoons coarsely chopped fresh rosemary
Extra-virgin olive oil for drizzling

◈ Lightly oil an 8-inch (20-cm) cake pan or similar pan. Place the dough in the prepared pan and gently stretch it to the edges, pulling it from the center outward to achieve an even thickness. If the dough springs back toward the center and is difficult to work with, cover and set it aside to relax for 10 minutes, then continue coaxing the dough out to an even thickness. Cover with a kitchen towel and let rise until almost doubled in bulk and very soft and puffy, about 45 minutes.

◈ Preheat an oven to 475°F (245°C).

◈ Using your fingertips, dimple the dough vigorously in several places, leaving indentations about ½ inch (12 mm) deep. Again cover the pan with a towel and let rise for 20 minutes longer.

◈ Sprinkle the risen dough evenly with the salt and pepper to taste and the rosemary. Drizzle with olive oil. Bake until golden brown and cooked through, 15–18 minutes. Transfer the pan to a rack and let stand until the focaccia is barely warm, about 10 minutes, then serve.

Makes one 8-inch (20-cm) focaccia round

Focaccia with Onion, Walnuts and Gorgonzola

Cut into thin slices or squares, this focaccia makes a marvelous addition to a simple antipasto accompanied with a glass of vino da tavola. *Gorgonzola dolcelatte, which is sweeter and milder than Gorgonzola piccante, can be found in well-stocked cheese shops. If Gorgonzola dolcelatte is unavailable, substitute crumbled Cambozola blue cheese.*

½ recipe herb-flavored focaccia dough *(recipe on page 13),* completed through the first rising

2 tablespoons extra-virgin olive oil

½ large yellow onion, thinly sliced

3 oz (90 g) Gorgonzola dolcelatte cheese, coarsely chopped

¼ cup (1 oz/30 g) coarsely chopped walnuts

Lightly oil an 8-inch (20-cm) cake pan or similar pan. Place the dough in the prepared pan and gently stretch it to the edges, pulling it from the center outward to achieve an even thickness. If the dough springs back toward the center and is difficult to work with, cover and set it aside to relax for 10 minutes, then continue coaxing the dough out to an even thickness. Cover with a kitchen towel and let rise until almost doubled in bulk and very soft and puffy, about 45 minutes.

While the dough is rising, in a sauté pan over medium-low heat, warm the olive oil. Add the onion and sauté until golden brown and very soft and sweet, about 20 minutes. Remove from the heat and let cool.

Preheat an oven to 475°F (245°C).

Using your fingertips, dimple the dough vigorously in several places, leaving indentations about ½ inch (12 mm) deep. Again cover the pan with a towel and let rise for 20 minutes longer.

Spread the cooked onion evenly over the risen dough, then scatter the Gorgonzola over the onion. Top with the walnuts. Bake until golden brown and cooked through, 15–18 minutes. Transfer the pan to a rack and let stand until the focaccia is barely warm, about 10 minutes, then serve.

Makes one 8-inch (20-cm) focaccia round

Seared Halibut Sandwich with Roasted Red Pepper and Arugula

The American love of substantial sandwiches meets traditional Italian flavors in this panino. It is the type of lunch fare found at many of the new and stylish American pizzerias.

½ red bell pepper (capsicum)
¼ lb (125 g) halibut fillet
1 tablespoon olive oil
   Salt and freshly ground pepper
2 tablespoons mayonnaise
1 teaspoon chopped fresh thyme
½ teaspoon Dijon mustard
   Focaccia with red onion *(recipe on page 72)*
½ cup (½ oz/15 g) loosely packed arugula (rocket) leaves
2 thin slices red (Spanish) onion
   Juice of ½ lemon

▣ Preheat a broiler (griller) or preheat an oven to 450°F (230°C). Remove the seeds and ribs from the pepper half and place, cut side down, on a baking sheet. Place in the broiler or oven and broil (grill) or bake until the skin is charred and blistered. Alternatively, using tongs or a fork, hold the pepper half over a gas flame until charred and blistered. Immediately place the pepper half in a bowl and cover tightly with plastic wrap. Let steam until cool, about 15 minutes. Using your fingers, peel off the charred skin. Cut lengthwise into narrow strips. Set aside.

▣ Preheat a gas grill or a ridged stove-top griddle on high, or place a heavy sauté pan (preferably cast iron) over medium-high heat until very hot. Brush the halibut fillet with the olive oil and season to taste with salt and pepper. Add the fish to the hot grill, griddle or sauté pan and cook, turning once, until nicely browned on both sides and opaque at the center, about 3 minutes on each side depending upon thickness.

▣ While the fish is cooking, in a small bowl, whisk together the mayonnaise, thyme and mustard until blended.

▣ Slice the focaccia in half horizontally. Cut the halibut into slices ½ inch (12 mm) thick. Spread the mustard mayonnaise on the cut sides of the focaccia. Distribute the arugula evenly over the bottom of the focaccia. Top evenly with the sliced halibut and then with the pepper strips and onion slices. Sprinkle with the lemon juice and salt and pepper to taste. Place the other half of the focaccia on top, cut side down, and press down firmly with the palm of your hand. Cut the *panino* in half or in quarters for easier eating and serve.

Makes 1 sandwich

Light Meals

The institution of the pizzeria continues to evolve with changing times and the changing tastes of its customers. In no aspect of the menu does this fact show more clearly than in the offerings of light meals.

Smart pizzeria owners know that not every customer will necessarily want to order a pizza. Many people, particularly time-pressed workers who want to grab a quick lunch or moviegoers looking for a bite to eat before a show, are in search of a convenient and satisfying one-dish meal, or *piatto unico.*

The *piatto unico* could be a rich soup brimming with vegetables and the comforting tenderness of rice, or a pasta dish sauced with fresh tomatoes highlighted by a drizzle of balsamic vinegar and piquant accents of capers and shallots. Daily specials on the menu might explore more adventurous territory—herbed, braised artichokes filled with a savory mixture of green lentils and chicken or a new version of the traditional Tuscan bread salad made with grilled slices of a country loaf and freshly cooked shrimp. Of necessity, dishes such as a roasted chicken cooked on a bed of potatoes or a robust lasagna oozing with the richness of four cheeses preserve a direct connection to traditional rustic tastes.

Roasted Chicken Sausages with Red Peppers

In small pizzerias, the forno a legna, *or "wood-fired pizza oven," is often used for preparing simple main courses such as this hearty dish of roasted sausages and peppers. It can also be made with traditional Italian sausages—with or without fennel, mild or highly spiced.*

8   chicken sausages

10 fresh thyme sprigs

2   tablespoons extra-virgin olive oil

1   large red (Spanish) onion, cut in half through the stem end and thinly sliced

3   cloves garlic, minced

4   red bell peppers (capsicums), seeded, deribbed and cut lengthwise into strips ¼ inch (6 mm) wide

¼   cup (⅓ oz/10 g) coarsely chopped fresh flat-leaf (Italian) parsley
    Salt and freshly ground pepper

◻ Preheat an oven to 450°F (230°C).

◻ Arrange the sausages in a roasting pan just large enough to hold them in a single layer. Tuck the thyme sprigs around them. Pour in water to a depth of ½ inch (12 mm). Roast, turning the sausages once or twice, until the water has completely evaporated and the sausages are nicely browned, 10–15 minutes.

◻ While the sausages are cooking, in a frying pan over medium-low heat, warm the olive oil. Add the onion and sauté, stirring occasionally, until limp, 5–6 minutes. Add the garlic and sauté for 1 minute longer. Stir in the bell peppers and sauté, stirring occasionally, until the peppers just begin to soften, about 10 minutes. Remove from the heat and set aside.

◻ When the sausages have browned, add the bell pepper mixture to the roasting pan along with the parsley and salt and pepper to taste. Return the roasting pan to the oven and continue to roast until the sausages are a deep golden brown and the vegetables are golden, about 15 minutes longer. Transfer to a warmed platter and serve immediately.

Serves 4–6

Summer Linguine

Summertime is made for exploring the abundant offerings at local farmers' markets. Look for small, tender Blue Lake beans or richly flavored flat romanos. Fresh zucchini flowers add their sunny color and subtle squash flavor to this light vegetarian dish.

¼ cup (2 fl oz/60 ml) extra-virgin olive oil, plus olive oil as needed

1 shallot, minced

2 cloves garlic, minced

2 russet or golden-fleshed potatoes, peeled and cut into small dice

1 zucchini (courgette), ends trimmed, cut in half lengthwise and then cut crosswise into half-moons

½ lb (250 g) green beans *(see note)*, ends trimmed and strings removed

¼ lb (250 g) zucchini (courgette) flowers, stamens removed, optional

¼ cup (⅓ oz/10 g) coarsely chopped fresh basil
    Salt and freshly ground pepper
    Juice of ½ lemon, or to taste

1 lb (500 g) dried Italian linguine

2 tablespoons unsalted butter, at room temperature
    Freshly grated Italian Parmesan cheese

▣ In a frying pan over medium-low heat, warm the ¼ cup (2 fl oz/60 ml) olive oil. Add the shallot and garlic and sauté for a few seconds, stirring frequently, just until the flavors are released. Add the potatoes and sauté, gently tossing once or twice, until just tender, about 7 minutes. Add the zucchini, green beans, zucchini flowers (if using) and basil. Continue sautéing, stirring occasionally, until all the vegetables are tender, about 10 minutes longer. Season to taste with salt, pepper and lemon juice.

▣ While the vegetables are cooking, fill a deep pot three-fourths full with lightly salted water and bring to a rolling boil. Add the pasta and stir a few times to prevent it from sticking together or to the pan. Cook until al dente, 7–8 minutes or according to the package directions. Scoop out and reserve ½ cup (4 fl oz/125 ml) of the cooking water. Drain the linguine thoroughly in a colander.

▣ Immediately place the sautéed vegetables with all their juices and the reserved cooking water in a large shallow pasta bowl. Add the linguine and butter, toss to mix well and serve immediately. Pass Parmesan cheese at the table.

Serves 4–6

Artichokes Stuffed with Chicken and Lentils

No one can meander the streets of Rome without coming under the spell of the purple-green spineless artichoke. In season one sees flatbed trucks laden with the long-stemmed beauties. Here, artichokes are cooked Roman style with herbs, stuffed with a savory filling and then briefly baked.

¼ cup (2 fl oz/60 ml) extra-virgin olive oil

½ cup (4 fl oz/125 ml) water

4 cloves garlic, minced

2 tablespoons coarsely chopped fresh flat-leaf (Italian) parsley

2 tablespoons coarsely chopped fresh basil

4 large artichokes, trimmed *(see glossary, page 124)* and halved lengthwise
 Salt and freshly ground pepper

CHICKEN AND LENTIL FILLING

½ cup (3½ oz/105 g) small green French lentils

2 tablespoons extra-virgin olive oil

3 cloves garlic, minced

10 oz (315 g) ground (minced) chicken breast meat

¼ cup (⅓ oz/10 g) coarsely chopped fresh flat-leaf (Italian) parsley
 Coarse salt and freshly ground pepper

½ cup (4 fl oz/125 ml) tomato-basil sauce *(recipe on page 14)*

 Lemon wedges, optional

¼ cup (⅓ oz/10 g) coarsely chopped fresh flat-leaf (Italian) parsley, optional

Place the olive oil and water in a frying pan just large enough to hold the 8 artichoke halves. Scatter the garlic and herbs in the pan and arrange the artichoke halves, cut sides down, in a circular pattern with the stems facing toward the center of the pan. Season to taste with salt and pepper. Place over medium-high heat, bring to a simmer, cover and cook until almost tender, about 10 minutes. Remove from the heat and set aside.

To make the filling, in a saucepan, bring a generous amount of lightly salted water to a boil. Add the lentils and reduce the heat so that the water simmers. Cook, uncovered, until the lentils are just tender but still hold their shape, 20–25 minutes. Drain and refresh them under cold running water to halt the cooking. Drain again and set aside.

In a frying pan over low heat, warm the olive oil. Add the garlic and cook gently, stirring frequently, until the garlic turns opaque, 3–4 seconds. Add the ground chicken, raise the heat to medium and sauté, stirring and breaking up the chicken with a wooden spoon so that it cooks evenly, until cooked through and no trace of pink remains, about 10 minutes. Remove from the heat and add the drained lentils, parsley and salt and pepper to taste. Pour in the tomato-basil sauce and toss gently to mix well.

Preheat an oven to 375°F (190°C).

Place the braised artichokes, hollow sides up, in a baking dish in which they fit in a single layer. Divide the filling mixture evenly among the halves, mounding it high for an attractive presentation. Bake until heated through, about 10 minutes.

Remove from the oven and serve the artichokes hot, cold or at room temperature, arranged on a platter or divided among individual plates. Garnish with lemon wedges and parsley, if desired.

Serves 4–6

Bread Salad with Grilled Shrimp

In many cultures where food traditions were formed amid great poverty, there is much ingenuity in the use of stale bread. Panzanella, a Tuscan salad of stale bread soaked in water, squeezed dry and tossed with a varied mix of ingredients, was created in this spirit. This version, which includes shrimp, would be at home on the menu of any contemporary American pizzeria.

4   tomatoes, cut into small dice

1   large cucumber, peeled, seeded and cut into small dice

2   bell peppers (capsicums), any color, seeded, deribbed and cut into small dice

1   shallot, minced

2   tablespoons capers, rinsed, drained and coarsely chopped

1   tablespoon coarsely chopped fresh oregano

¼   cup (⅓ oz/10 g) fresh flat-leaf (Italian) parsley

¼   cup (2 fl oz/60 ml) extra-virgin olive oil, plus olive oil for drizzling on bread

2   tablespoons red wine vinegar

24   large shrimp (prawns), peeled and deveined

    Olive oil for brushing

3   thick slices country-style bread

1   clove garlic

    Salt and freshly ground pepper

    Lemon wedges

◻ In a large serving bowl, combine the tomatoes, cucumber, bell peppers, shallot, capers, oregano and parsley. Add the ¼ cup (2 fl oz/60 ml) extra-virgin olive oil and the vinegar, toss to mix and set aside for at least 1 hour or up to 6 hours.

◻ Prepare a fire in a charcoal grill or preheat a ridged stove-top griddle until it is very hot.

◻ Lightly brush the shrimp with olive oil. Place the shrimp on the grill rack 7–8 inches (18–20 cm) above the fire or on the griddle and cook, turning once, until pink and cooked through, about 6 minutes total. Remove the shrimp from the grill or griddle and toss into the bowl with the prepared vegetables.

◻ Place the bread slices on the grill rack or griddle and grill, turning once, until grill marks are apparent on both sides and the bread is toasted, 3–4 minutes total. Remove the bread from the grill or griddle and quickly rub one side of each slice with the garlic clove. Drizzle a little extra-virgin olive oil over the bread.

◻ Let the bread cool, then tear into 2-inch (5-cm) pieces. Add to the shrimp and vegetables. Season to taste with salt and pepper and toss to mix well.

◻ Divide evenly among individual plates and garnish with lemon wedges. Serve immediately.

Serves 4–6

Chick-pea Soup with Swiss Chard and Tomatoes

Chick-peas and Swiss chard both have an earthy nuttiness that is particularly suited to creating full-flavored vegetarian soups. This soup is brothy; to make a thicker zuppa, *put half the cooked vegetables through a food mill fitted with the coarse disk. To enrich the presentation of the soup, ladle it over a large* crostino *placed in the bottom of each bowl.*

2 tablespoons extra-virgin olive oil
1 yellow onion, coarsely chopped
3 cloves garlic, minced
8 small plum (Roma) tomatoes, coarsely chopped
1 bunch Swiss chard (silverbeet)
1 can (16 oz/500 g) chick-peas (garbanzo beans), drained
6 cups (48 fl oz/1.5 l) water
   Salt and freshly ground pepper

In a heavy soup pot over medium heat, warm the olive oil. Add the onion and sauté, stirring frequently, until wilted but not browned, 3–4 minutes. Add the garlic and stir for a few seconds. Then add the tomatoes, raise the heat to medium-high and cook, stirring occasionally, just until the tomatoes begin to break down and form a sauce, about 10 minutes.

While the tomatoes are cooking, cut off and discard the bottom third of the Swiss chard stems. Cut the remaining stem portions crosswise into pieces ¼ inch (6 mm) wide. Working with several chard leaves at a time, stack them, roll them up lengthwise and then cut crosswise to form ribbons ¼ inch (6 mm) wide.

Add the chard, chick-peas and water to the soup pot and bring to a simmer over medium-high heat. Cook uncovered, adjusting the heat as necessary to maintain a simmer, until the vegetables are tender and the flavors have blended, 30–45 minutes. The soup will be brothy and chunky.

Season to taste with salt and pepper. Ladle the soup into shallow bowls and serve at once.

Serves 4

Orecchiette with Tomato-Shallot Sauce

Roman cooks are famous for hot pasta tossed in a mixture of chopped raw tomatoes, garlic, basil and oil. Variations on this easy, tasty and colorful base are now found all over Italy. Since the ingredients are already on hand for pizza making, this light, refreshing dish is a welcome addition to a pizzeria menu, especially on warm summer nights.

10	ripe yet firm plum (Roma) tomatoes, chopped
2	shallots, minced
2	cloves garlic, minced
1–2	tablespoons capers, rinsed, drained and coarsely chopped
¼	cup (2 fl oz/60 ml) balsamic vinegar
½–1	cup (4–8 fl oz/125–250 ml) extra-virgin olive oil
	Small handful of coarsely chopped fresh flat-leaf (Italian) parsley
10	fresh basil leaves, chopped
	Salt and freshly ground pepper
1	lb (500 g) Italian orecchiette

In a large, shallow pasta bowl, combine the tomatoes, shallots, garlic, capers, vinegar, ½ cup (4 fl oz/ 125 ml) olive oil, parsley, basil, and salt and pepper to taste. For a fuller, richer flavor, add all or part of the remaining ½ cup (4 fl oz/125 ml) olive oil, if desired. Toss well, cover and set aside in a cool place for at least 1 hour or for up to 3 hours.

When ready to serve, fill a deep pot three-fourths full with lightly salted water and bring to a rolling boil. Add the pasta and stir a few times to prevent it from sticking together or to the pan. Cook until al dente, 7–10 minutes or according to the package directions. Drain the pasta thoroughly in a colander and add it to the serving bowl with the sauce mixture. Toss well and serve immediately.

Serves 4–6

Lasagna with Four Cheeses

*Few baked pastas are as rich and satisfying as this dish from northern Italy. The new
"no-boil" lasagna sheets have a marvelous tender texture, although it is wise to dip them briefly
in boiling water for the best result. Regular lasagna noodles can also be used.*

BÉCHAMEL SAUCE

3½	cups (28 fl oz/875 ml) milk
1	fresh rosemary sprig, 2 inches (5 cm) long
6	tablespoons (3 oz/90 g) unsalted butter
5	tablespoons (1½ oz/45 g) all-purpose (plain) flour
	Salt and freshly ground pepper

GARLIC BREAD CRUMBS

1	loaf good-quality country-style bread, about ½ lb (250 g), cut into 1-inch (2.5-cm) cubes
1	tablespoon minced garlic, or to taste
	Salt and freshly ground pepper
	Extra-virgin olive oil, as needed
½	cup (2 oz/60 g) walnuts
1½	cups (12 oz/375 g) ricotta cheese
¾	cup (6 oz/185 g) mascarpone cheese
¾	cup (3 oz/90 g) shredded Fontina cheese
2	cups (8 oz/250 g) freshly grated Italian Parmesan cheese
1	tablespoon minced fresh rosemary
3	tablespoons chopped fresh flat-leaf (Italian) parsley
	Salt and freshly ground pepper
20	sheets "no-boil" lasagna

▣ To make the béchamel sauce, pour the milk into a saucepan, add the rosemary sprig and place over medium-low heat until small bubbles appear along the pan edge. In a small saucepan over medium-low heat, melt the butter. Add the flour and whisk to form a smooth paste. Reduce the heat to low and cook, stirring, for about 2 minutes. When the milk is hot, add the butter-flour mixture, whisking constantly. Simmer over medium heat until the sauce thickens enough to coat a spoon, about 20 minutes. Remove and discard the rosemary sprig. Season to taste with salt and pepper. Set aside to cool.

▣ To make the bread crumbs, preheat an oven to 350°F (180°C). In a food processor fitted with the metal blade, pulse the bread cubes to produce coarse crumbs. In a large bowl, combine the crumbs, garlic and salt and pepper to taste. Add enough olive oil to moisten the mixture slightly. Spread on a baking sheet and bake until barely golden, 2–4 minutes.

▣ Spread the walnuts on a baking sheet and toast until golden and fragrant, about 10 minutes. Let cool. Raise the oven temperature to 375°F (190°C). In a large bowl, combine the toasted walnuts, ricotta, mascarpone, Fontina, 1 cup (4 oz/125 g) of the Parmesan, rosemary, parsley, and salt and pepper to taste. Mix well. Add 1 cup (8 fl oz/250 ml) of the béchamel and stir vigorously to mix.

▣ Fill a deep pot three-fourths full with lightly salted water and bring to a rolling boil. Using tongs, dip the "no-boil" lasagna sheets into the boiling water for 10 seconds, then lay them on a kitchen towel to drain.

▣ Spread a thin layer of béchamel over the bottom of a 13-by-9-by-2-inch (33-by-23-by-5-cm) lasagna pan. Top with a layer of pasta, then with a layer of the cheese mixture. Top with a layer ¼ inch (6 mm) thick of the béchamel. Sprinkle with 1 tablespoon of the remaining Parmesan. Top with another layer of pasta sheets. Alternate layers of the cheese mixture and béchamel and Parmesan, until all the ingredients except the Parmesan are used up, ending with béchamel. Scatter the remaining Parmesan and the bread crumbs over the top. Cover and bake until the dish is bubbling, 35–40 minutes. Uncover and bake until the bread crumbs are crunchy, about 10 minutes longer. Let stand for 5–10 minutes before serving.

Serves 6–8

Wild Mushroom Soup

In Umbria, a region in the heart of Italy, soups are often made from an extraordinary assortment of mushrooms that have been gathered by families on Sunday outings in the woods. In this recipe, a mixture of cultivated pale brown cremini and white mushrooms are used. Feel free to substitute any full-flavored fresh mushrooms, cultivated or wild, including chanterelles, morels and porcini.

⅓   cup (2 oz/60 g) pine nuts

½   cup (4 fl oz/125 ml) extra-virgin olive oil

1   large yellow onion, finely chopped

3   cloves garlic, minced

10 plum (Roma) tomatoes, chopped

1   lb (500 g) fresh shiitake mushrooms, stems removed, sliced

½   lb (250 g) fresh cremini or white mushrooms, stems removed, sliced

6   cups (48 fl oz/1.5 l) water

1   tablespoon chopped fresh basil

1   tablespoon chopped fresh flat-leaf (Italian) parsley

1   tablespoon chopped fresh rosemary

1   tablespoon chopped fresh thyme
    Salt and freshly ground pepper

◾ Preheat an oven to 350°F (180°C). Spread the pine nuts on a baking sheet and toast until golden and fragrant, 5–8 minutes. Remove from the oven and let cool.

◾ In a heavy soup pot over medium heat, warm the olive oil. Add the onion and sauté, stirring frequently, until soft and golden, about 5 minutes. Add the garlic, tomatoes and mushrooms and raise the heat to high. Sauté, stirring often, just until the mushrooms begin to release their liquid, about 7 minutes.

◾ Add the water and herbs and bring to a boil. Reduce the heat to medium-low and simmer uncovered, stirring occasionally, until all the vegetables are tender and the flavors are blended, 25–30 minutes. Season to taste with salt and pepper. Ladle into warmed shallow soup bowls, scatter the pine nuts evenly over the tops and serve immediately.

Serves 4–6

Spinach-Ricotta Dumplings with Red Pepper Sauce

These light dumplings are made from the filling commonly used in stuffing ravioli.
They are called ravioli nudi, *"naked ravioli," because they lack a pasta covering.*

RED PEPPER SAUCE

4   large, fleshy red bell peppers (capsicums)
2   tablespoons unsalted butter
2   tablespoons extra-virgin olive oil
½   small yellow onion, cut into small dice
2   cloves garlic
1   cup (8 fl oz/250 ml) water or chicken or vegetable stock
¼   cup (⅓ oz/10 g) coarsely chopped fresh flat-leaf (Italian) parsley
5   fresh basil leaves
     Salt and freshly ground pepper
2   tablespoons heavy (double) cream, optional

3   bunches spinach, about 1 lb (500 g) each, stems removed
3   eggs, lightly beaten
¾   cup (3 oz/90 g) freshly grated Italian Parmesan cheese, plus cheese for garnishing
¾   cup (3 oz/90 g) freshly grated pecorino romano cheese
2   cups (1 lb/500 g) ricotta cheese
3   tablespoons unbleached all-purpose (plain) flour, plus flour for dredging
1   teaspoon salt
¼   teaspoon freshly ground pepper
2   tablespoons unsalted butter, melted
½   cup (4 oz/125 g) unsalted butter
10   fresh sage leaves

▣ To make the pepper sauce, use a vegetable peeler to remove the thin skin from the peppers. Cut each in half lengthwise and pull out and discard the stem, seeds and ribs. Cut the peppers lengthwise into strips.

▣ In a sauté pan over medium heat, melt the butter with the olive oil. Add the onion and cook, stirring occasionally, until golden, about 7 minutes. Add the garlic and bell peppers and sauté, stirring occasionally, until the peppers soften, about 10 minutes. Add the water or stock, parsley and basil and bring to a simmer. Simmer, uncovered, until the peppers are tender, about 10 minutes longer. Season to taste with salt and pepper. Purée the pepper mixture in a blender or in a food processor fitted with the metal blade and transfer to a bowl. Stir in the cream, if using.

▣ Rinse the spinach but do not dry. Place in a large saucepan over medium-low heat, cover and cook, turning occasionally, until wilted, 2–4 minutes. Drain, squeeze to remove the liquid and chop finely. In a bowl, combine the spinach, eggs, ¾ cup (3 oz/90 g) each of the Parmesan and pecorino romano cheeses, ricotta cheese, 3 tablespoons flour, salt and pepper. Stir well until the mixture resembles a thick, slightly stiff batter. Add flour to a shallow dish to a depth of ½ inch (12 mm). Form the ricotta mixture into balls about ¾ inch (2 cm) in diameter. Roll them lightly in the flour, coating evenly, and place them on a lightly floured tray.

▣ Preheat an oven to 250°F (120°C). Fill a deep pot three-fourths full with lightly salted water and bring to a gentle simmer. Add the dumplings a few at a time. Nudge them occasionally to ensure that they cook evenly. The dumplings are ready when they rise to the surface and then cook for another minute or so; this will take about 3 minutes in all. Lift out the dumplings and drain thoroughly on an absorbent kitchen towel. Place in an ovenproof dish, drizzle with the 2 tablespoons melted butter and cover to keep warm.

▣ Meanwhile, in a saucepan over medium heat, warm the pepper purée. In a sauté pan over high heat, melt the ½ cup (4 oz/125 g) butter. Add the sage leaves and sauté, stirring frequently, until the sage leaves are crispy, about 5 minutes. Transfer to paper towels to drain.

▣ Pour the purée onto individual plates and place the dumplings on top. Spoon on the sage leaves and some of the butter. Dust with Parmesan cheese.

Serves 4–6

Roasted Chicken with Potatoes

Nearly every casual Italian dining establishment offers roasted chicken. In this version,
a paste of caramelized garlic and herbs is slathered over the chicken to create a savory crust.

20 cloves garlic
    Olive oil, to cover
1   tablespoon chopped fresh
    oregano, plus oregano sprigs for
    garnish
1   tablespoon chopped fresh thyme
    leaves, plus thyme sprigs for
    garnish
2   tablespoons hot water
2   small chickens, about 2 lb (1 kg)
    each
    Salt and freshly ground pepper
6   russet or golden-fleshed potatoes,
    peeled and thinly sliced
2   yellow onions, thinly sliced
    Lemon wedges

◈ Peel the garlic but leave the cloves whole. In a small, heavy saucepan over medium-low heat, combine the garlic cloves with olive oil just to cover. Bring to a gentle simmer and cook the garlic until it is covered with golden dots, about 15 minutes. Watch carefully, as the garlic burns easily. Remove from the heat, let cool and then drain off the oil. Set the oil aside.

◈ In a blender or in a food processor fitted with the metal blade, combine the garlic cloves, chopped oregano and thyme, hot water and a little of the reserved oil, if desired. Purée to form a coarse paste, scraping down the sides of the blender or bowl as necessary. Transfer to a small bowl. Set aside.

◈ Preheat an oven to 400°F (200°C).

◈ Using poultry shears or a heavy knife, cut the chickens in half lengthwise. Cut out and discard the backbone. Season the chickens generously with salt and pepper and let stand at room temperature for 10 minutes.

◈ Rub the garlic paste generously over the chickens, coating all the surfaces. Place the potatoes in an even layer in a roasting pan just large

enough to hold the chickens comfortably in a single layer. Top the potatoes with the onions, distributing them evenly, then season with salt and pepper. Drizzle with a bit of the reserved garlic oil; reserve the remaining oil for another use. Lay the chickens, cut sides down, on top of the vegetables and cover the pan with aluminum foil.

◈ Roast until the chickens begin to brown, 20–30 minutes. Raise the oven temperature to 450°F (230°C). Remove the foil and baste the chickens with the accumulated pan juices. Continue to roast, uncovered, until crusty and deep golden brown and the juices run clear when a thigh is pierced, 10–15 minutes longer.

◈ Transfer the chicken and potatoes to a large platter and garnish with lemon wedges and thyme and oregano sprigs.

Serves 4–6

Desserts

Apart from the innate appeal of their food, pizzerias are patronized for their reasonable prices and small, easy-to-comprehend menus. These qualities make it all the more crucial for the pizzeria chef to devise desserts that are simple and economical while also being as delicious as the foods that precede them.

To that end, most pizzerias offer a limited selection of sure-to-please items on the *carta dei dolci,* or "dessert menu." One might be a hand-beaten *granita di cappuccino,* "cappuccino ice," that is easily prepared even by someone with the most rudimentary of cooking skills. A trip to a nearby pastry shop might be in order, so that the pizzeria can offer something a bit more elegant like a *gianduia* tart featuring the popular combination of hazelnuts and chocolate. A special biscotti recipe is often contributed by a relative, the crisp twice-baked cookies served alongside steaming cups of espresso or cappuccino.

Other items prepared on the premises fall into the category of *dolci al cucchiaio,* "spoon desserts," like a creamy pudding made with Arborio rice, or seasonal fruit such as peaches that can be quickly poached on the stove top while the busy cook prepares other dishes in the wood-fired pizza oven.

Caramelized Rice Pudding

Rice pudding is considered a homey treat in Italy, particularly in the north where it is made with the locally grown short-grained Arborio rice. This high-quality rice, generally used for making risotto, results in an especially creamy pudding. The caramelized topping adds a sweet crunch.

3 tablespoons dark rum

1 tablespoon water

⅓ cup (2 oz/60 g) raisins

½ cup (3½ oz/105 g) Arborio rice

2½ cups (20 fl oz/625 ml) half-and-half (half cream), or more if needed

½ vanilla bean, split lengthwise

2 egg yolks

½ cup (4 oz/120 g) sugar

¾ cup (6 fl oz/180 ml) heavy (double) cream

6 figs, cut in half through the stem end

In a small saucepan, combine the rum and water and bring to a boil. Remove from the heat, stir in the raisins and let stand until needed.

In the top pan of a double boiler, combine the rice, 2½ cups (20 fl oz/625 ml) half-and-half and vanilla bean. Bring water in the lower pan to a gentle boil; place the top pan over it (the pan should not touch the water). Cover and cook until the liquid is absorbed and the rice is tender, about 1 hour. Check the level of the liquid occasionally to make sure the pan does not go dry. If the rice is still a bit tough and all the liquid has been absorbed, add a little more half-and-half and cook until the rice softens. The rice mixture should be very thick.

Remove the top pan, uncover and set aside to cool for 5 minutes. Combine the yolks and ¼ cup (2 oz/60 g) of the sugar in a small bowl and whisk to blend. Whisk in a small amount of the rice mixture to warm the yolk mixture slightly, then whisk the yolk mixture into the rice mixture. Reposition the top pan over the lower pan of gently simmering water and cook uncovered, stirring occasionally, until thickened, 3–4 minutes. Remove the top pan and transfer the contents to a bowl. Cover with plastic wrap pressed directly onto the surface of the rice to prevent a skin from forming. Refrigerate until completely chilled. (The rice can be prepared to this stage up to 1 day before serving.)

In a bowl, whip the heavy cream until stiff peaks form. Remove and discard the vanilla bean from the rice pudding. Drain the raisins. Using a rubber spatula, fold the cream and the raisins into the rice mixture, distributing the raisins evenly and folding only until no white drifts of cream remain. Pack the pudding firmly into six ½-cup (4–fl oz/125-ml) flameproof ramekins. Level the surface, cover and refrigerate until well chilled before serving.

To serve, preheat a broiler (griller). Place the ramekins on a baking sheet. Divide the remaining ¼ cup (2 oz/60 g) sugar evenly among the ramekins, sprinkling 2 teaspoons of it evenly over the surface of each pudding. Place the ramekins in the broiler about 2 inches (5 cm) from the heat and broil (grill) until the sugar caramelizes, 2–3 minutes. Rotate the ramekins as needed so they brown evenly. Serve immediately, accompanied with the figs.

Serves 6

Hazelnut Tart

The flavor combination of hazelnuts and chocolate is a longtime Italian favorite and is so ubiquitous that it has its own name, gianduia. *The mixture is used in candy, ice cream and biscotti and in tarts such as this one, which might be found on the pastry cart of an upscale pizzeria.*

TART PASTRY
1   cup (5 oz/155 g) hazelnuts (filberts)
1   cup (5 oz/155 g) unbleached all-purpose (plain) flour
¼   cup (2 oz/60 g) sugar
6   tablespoons (3 oz/90 g) unsalted butter, melted

HAZELNUT FILLING
6   tablespoons (3 oz/90 g) cream cheese, at room temperature
½   cup (4 oz/125 g) ricotta cheese
5   tablespoons (2½ oz/75 g) sugar
1½ tablespoons Dutch-process cocoa
2   egg yolks plus 1 whole egg
1½ tablespoons Frangelico (hazelnut liqueur)
½   cup (2½ oz/75 g) coarsely chopped bittersweet chocolate

◼ To make the pastry, preheat an oven to 325°F (165°C). Spread the hazelnuts in a single layer on a baking sheet and place in the oven until they just begin to change color and the skins begin to loosen, 8–10 minutes. Spread the warm nuts on a kitchen towel. Cover with another kitchen towel and rub against the nuts to remove as much of the skins as possible. Let cool, then set aside ¾ cup (4 oz/125 g) of the nuts to use for the filling. Finely chop the remaining nuts and place in a bowl. Raise the oven temperature to 350°F (180°C).

◼ Add the flour and sugar to the chopped hazelnuts and stir to mix. Pour in the melted butter and stir to distribute evenly. The pastry dough should be moist but still crumbly. Transfer the dough into a 9-inch (23-cm) tart pan with a removable bottom and, using your fingertips, press it evenly over the bottom and sides of the pan. Chill for 15 minutes.

◼ Remove the pastry-lined pan from the refrigerator and line with a sheet of aluminum foil or parchment (baking) paper. Fill with pie weights or dried beans. Bake the pastry until the bottom is just set, about 15 minutes. Remove from the oven and remove the weights or beans and the foil or paper. Return the pastry to the oven and continue to bake until the pastry is lightly golden and pulls away from the sides of the pan, about 5 minutes longer. Transfer to a rack to cool completely.

◼ While the tart is cooling, make the filling: In a food processor fitted with the metal blade, combine the cream cheese, ricotta cheese, sugar and cocoa. Process until very smooth, stopping to scrape down the sides of the bowl as needed. Add the egg yolks and whole egg and again process until smooth. Add the Frangelico and pulse again just to blend.

◼ Pour the filling into the tart shell and jiggle the pan to level the filling. Coarsely chop the reserved hazelnuts and scatter them evenly over the surface along with the chocolate. Bake until the center is just set, 25–30 minutes. Transfer to a rack and let cool before serving.

Makes one 9-inch (23-cm) tart; serves 8–10

Vanilla Ice Cream with Strawberries and Balsamic Vinegar

Many small pizzerias lack the facilities for making elaborate desserts. They instead rely on dolci al cucchiaio, *or "spoon desserts," that can be prepared quickly with easily available ingredients. In this popular, rich summertime spoon dessert, piquant balsamic vinegar flavors fresh strawberries and ice cream.*

1	pt (500 ml) vanilla ice cream
2½	cups (10 oz/315 g) strawberries, stems removed, halved lengthwise
¼	cup (2 fl oz/60 ml) balsamic vinegar, or to taste
1	tablespoon sugar
	Coarsely ground pepper

▩ Remove the ice cream from the freezer and let stand at room temperature until it is soft enough to stir into the strawberries, 10–15 minutes, depending upon on how cold the freezer is.

▩ Meanwhile, in a bowl large enough to accommodate the ice cream eventually, stir together the strawberries, ¼ cup (2 fl oz/60 ml) balsamic vinegar, sugar and pepper to taste. The vinegar and sugar will mix with the berries' natural juices to create a sauce-like consistency. Taste and add more vinegar if needed.

▩ When the ice cream is soft enough, add it to the berry mixture. Immediately stir together until the berries and ice cream are evenly distributed. Spoon into tall wineglasses and serve at once.

Serves 4

Chocolate Biscotti

Although it would be unlikely to find biscotti served in a traditional pizzeria in the historic center of Naples, they are common in the pizzerias popular today. These delicious cookies are rich with chocolaty flavor and not too sweet and have the perfect consistency for dipping. The almonds add extra crunch.

¼ cup (1½ oz/45 g) whole blanched almonds

3 tablespoons unsalted butter, at room temperature

½ cup (4 oz/125 g) sugar

1 egg

½ teaspoon pure vanilla extract (essence)

¾ cup (4 oz/125 g) all-purpose (plain) flour

¼ cup (¾ oz/20 g) sifted Dutch-process cocoa

½ teaspoon baking powder

⅛ teaspoon baking soda (bicarbonate of soda)

2 oz (60 g) semisweet or bittersweet chocolate, coarsely chopped

◫ Preheat an oven to 400°F (200°C). Spread the almonds in a single layer on a baking sheet. Place in the oven until lightly toasted and fragrant, about 7 minutes. Remove from the oven and let cool. Reduce the oven temperature to 350°F (180°C).

◫ Line the bottom of a large baking sheet with parchment (baking) paper or aluminum foil. Nest the paper-lined sheet in a second baking sheet of the same size; this will prevent the bottoms of the cookies from scorching.

◫ In a large bowl, using a wooden spoon, cream together the butter and sugar until light and fluffy. Add the egg and vanilla and beat well. Set aside.

◫ In a food processor fitted with the metal blade, combine the flour, cocoa, baking powder and baking soda. Pulse briefly to combine, then add the chopped chocolate. Process continuously until the chocolate is finely and evenly chopped. Add the flour mixture to the butter mixture and blend just until combined. The mixture should come together into a soft dough. Add the almonds and mix until evenly distributed.

◫ On a lightly floured work surface, use your hands to shape the dough into a log about 13 inches (33 cm) long and 2½ inches (6 cm) in diameter. Place the log on the prepared baking sheet. Bake until the edges are firm (the center will not seem done yet), 30–35 minutes.

◫ Remove from the oven and let cool until lukewarm, about 30 minutes. Reduce the oven temperature to 300°F (150°C). Slice the log crosswise on a slight diagonal into pieces ¾ inch (2 cm) wide and return to the baking sheet, cut sides down. Bake for 10 minutes. Turn the cookies over and bake until lightly toasted, about 10 minutes longer. Remove from the oven, transfer to a rack and let cool completely. Store in an airtight container for up to 1 month. The biscotti can actually be stored for up to 6 months, if you can keep your hands out of the container. If they have become soft, recrisp them in a 350°F (180°C) oven for 5–6 minutes.

Makes 15–18 cookies

Peaches Poached in Wine

One of the wonders of summer, peaches are showcased in this easy dessert. The amount of sugar added to the poaching liquid will depend upon the wine's relative dryness; the liquid should be just sweet enough to heighten the natural sweetness of the peaches. To dress up the dish, top each serving with a dollop of mascarpone.

6   yellow- or white-fleshed peaches
1   bottle (24 fl oz/750 ml) fruity white or red wine or Champagne
⅓–⅔ cup (3–5 oz/90–155 g) sugar
1   vanilla bean, split lengthwise

▥ Bring a saucepan three-fourths full of water to a boil. One at a time, dip each peach into the boiling water for 5 seconds. Lift out with a slotted spoon and, using a sharp paring knife, peel the peaches. Halve each fruit along the natural line and remove the pits.

▥ In a saucepan large enough to hold all the peaches in a single layer, combine the wine, ⅓ cup (3 oz/90 g) sugar and vanilla bean. Place over low heat and stir until the sugar dissolves. Taste and add more sugar as needed to achieve a pleasant sweetness (see note). Bring to a simmer, add the peaches and simmer until barely tender, 2–5 minutes, depending upon their ripeness.

▥ Transfer the peaches and their cooking liquid to a deep glass bowl (the peaches should be completely covered by the liquid) and let cool to room temperature. Cover tightly with plastic wrap and refrigerate for at least 2 days or for up to 3 days.

▥ To serve, using a slotted spoon, transfer the peach halves to large wineglasses, placing 2 halves in each glass. Half-fill each glass with the poaching liquid and serve.

Serves 6

Cappuccino Ice

*In this day of complex appliances, it is good to be reminded that delicious desserts
can be made with just a bowl and a whisk. It is just this type of quick-to-assemble granita
that can be tended to easily in between the more demanding culinary tasks in a pizzeria.
For a special treat, accompany the ice with chocolate biscotti (recipe on page 117).*

2½ cups (20 fl oz/625 ml) hot
brewed espresso or brewed
French- or Italian-roast coffee

5–6 tablespoons (2½–3 oz/75–90 g)
sugar

½ cup (4 fl oz/125 ml) half-and-
half (half cream) or milk
Unsweetened whipped cream
Chocolate shavings

▣ In a 2½-qt (2.5-l) stainless-steel bowl, combine the hot espresso or coffee and 5 tablespoons (2½ oz/ 75 g) sugar and stir until the sugar is completely dissolved. Add the half-and-half or milk and mix well. Taste and add the remaining 1 tablespoon sugar if desired. Refrigerate until cold, then place, uncovered, in the freezer.

▣ When ice crystals have started to form around the edges, after 30–40 minutes, whisk the mixture vigorously to blend in the crystals. Return the bowl to the freezer and whisk again every 20–30 minutes until the mixture is a mass of coarse ice crystals yet still soft enough to spoon, 2–3 hours total. (If you forget the granita in the freezer and it hardens too much, let stand at room temperature for a few minutes, then whisk it to the correct consistency.)

▣ To serve, divide the ice among small serving bowls. Top each serving with a dollop of whipped cream and some chocolate shavings.

Serves 4–6

Sweet Pizza with Fruit and Almonds

A pizzeria sometimes pairs standard dough with sweet toppings to create a rustic dessert. In this example of that tradition, the intense heat of the hot pizza stone helps the ingredients to caramelize quickly and results in a homey dish that is creamy yet not too rich.

Neapolitan pizza dough *(recipe on page 12),* completed through the second rising

All-purpose (plain) flour for dusting

1 cup (8 oz/250 g) mascarpone cheese

2 teaspoons plus 2 tablespoons sugar

2 egg yolks

2 baking apples such as Granny Smith or Gravenstein, halved, cored and thinly sliced

1 pear, halved, cored and thinly sliced

2 tablespoons coarsely chopped almonds

Place a pizza stone or unglazed terra-cotta tiles on the lowest rack of an oven. Preheat to 475°F (245°C).

Cut each ball of dough into 2 equal pieces so that you have 4 balls. One at a time, place the balls on a lightly floured work surface and flatten slightly. Sprinkle a little flour on the top of the dough and, using your fingertips, press evenly until the ball is shaped into a round, flat disk. Gently lift the dough and stretch and rotate it until it is about ¼ inch (6 mm) thick and 6 inches (15 cm) in diameter. Alternatively, using a rolling pin, gently roll out each ball into a round 6 inches (15 cm) in diameter. Try not to let the center of the disks become too thin in comparison to the edges. Gently lay the dough rounds on a lightly floured pizza peel or rimless baking sheet.

In a small bowl, stir together the mascarpone, 2 teaspoons sugar and egg yolks until evenly blended. Spread the mixture over the pizza rounds, dividing it evenly and leaving about 1 inch (2.5 cm) uncovered at the edges. Arrange the apple and pear slices attractively on the rounds, dividing evenly and overlapping the slices slightly. Sprinkle the rounds with the remaining 2 tablespoons sugar and the almonds. Quickly slide the pizzas onto the preheated stone or tiles.

Bake until the edges of the dough are golden brown and the sugar is slightly caramelized, 15–18 minutes. Using a large metal spatula, remove the pizzas from the oven. Slide each pizza onto an individual dessert plate and serve immediately. Alternatively, transfer to a cutting board, cut each pizza in half and serve on individual serving plates.

Makes four 6-inch (15-cm) pizzas; serves 4 or 8

Glossary

The following glossary defines common ingredients and cooking terms, as well as special cooking equipment, used in pizzerias.

Anchovy Fillets

Fished in the waters that surround Italy, the tiny anchovy, a relative of the sardine, adds its intense, briny taste to pizzas and other pizzeria dishes. Anchovies are commonly sold as canned fillets that have been salted and packed in oil. Imported anchovy fillets in olive oil are the best, most widely available choice for the recipes in this book.

Artichokes

These large flower buds of a variety of thistle, also known as globe artichokes, are native to the Mediterranean. When large, the tight cluster of tough, pointed leaves covers pale green inner leaves and a gray-green base; together they make up the heart, which conceals a prickly choke. Italians prize baby artichokes (below) about 1½ inches (4 cm) in diameter.

TO TRIM ARTICHOKES

For baby artichokes, pull off the tough outer leaves from each artichoke. Trim the stem even with the base and cut away the fibrous, dark green layer around the base, being careful not to trim the rich meaty crown that lies beneath it. Cut off about 1 inch (2.5 cm) from the top.

For large artichokes, cut off about 2 inches (5 cm) from the top of each artichoke. Cut in half lengthwise and use a small, sharp-edged spoon to remove the fuzzy choke. Remove any interior leaves that have prickly tips. To prevent the artichokes from discoloring, rub the cut surfaces with a lemon half and immerse the trimmed artichokes in a bowl of water containing lemon juice.

Arugula

Also known as rocket, this green leaf vegetable has slender, multiple-lobed leaves and a peppery, slightly bitter flavor. Used raw in salads and *panini* and for topping pizzas.

Bell Peppers

These sweet, bell-shaped red, yellow or green peppers, also known as capsicums, had found their way from the New World into Italian kitchens by the 16th century. Before use, peppers must have their indigestible seeds removed.

Bread

To serve with authentic pizzeria-style meals, or for bread crumbs, choose a good country-style loaf made from unbleached wheat flour, with a firm, coarse crumb; also sometimes labeled "rustic" or "peasant-style" loaves.

TO MAKE BREAD CRUMBS

When a recipe calls for dried bread crumbs, first make fresh bread crumbs. Cut away the crusts from the bread and break the bread into coarse chunks. Place the chunks in a food processor fitted with the metal blade or in a blender and process to the desired consistency, usually fine or coarse. To dry the crumbs, spread them in a baking pan and leave in an oven set at its lowest temperature until they feel very dry, 30–60 minutes; do not allow them to brown. Store the crumbs in a covered container at room temperature. Fine dried bread crumbs may also be bought in food stores.

Capers

The buds of a common Mediterranean bush, capers grow wild throughout Italy. For use as a savory flavoring ingredient, they are first preserved in salt or, more commonly, are pickled in salt and vinegar.

Cheeses

Many different cheeses are produced in Italy. Among the most popular varieties, used in this book, are:

Fontina A creamy, delicate cow's milk cheese noted for its slightly nutty taste. Fontina from the Aosta Valley of northwestern Italy is generally considered the best.

Goat Generally soft, fresh and creamy, goat's milk cheeses are notable for their mild tang. Sold in small rounds or logs, they are used in antipasti, pizza toppings and other pizza fare.

Gorgonzola Dolcelatte Literally "sweet milk Gorgonzola," this cheese is a milder variety of the popular creamy, pale yellow, blue-veined cheese of Lombardy.

Mascarpone A thick, fresh cream cheese traditionally sold in small tubs. Similar to French crème fraîche, it is used to enrich sauces or desserts, and may also be sweetened and flavored for eating on its own.

Mozzarella An essential pizza topping, this mild, rindless white cheese is traditionally made from water buffalo's milk and sold fresh. Commercially produced and packaged cow's milk mozzarella, more commonly available, has a firmer consistency and is recommended for the pizza recipes in this book. Fresh mozzarella is sold immersed in water and should be drained before using. Mozzarella may also be flavored and preserved by smoking, giving it a sturdier texture and a deep yellowish brown color.

Parmesan With a sharp, salty, full flavor acquired during at least 2 years of aging, the best examples of this hard, thick-crusted cow's milk cheese are prized among cooks and diners alike. Although it takes its name from the city of Parma, Parmesan originated midway between that city and Reggio, where the finest variety, Parmigiano-Reggiano®, is produced. Buy in block form, to grate fresh as needed.

Pecorino Sheep's milk cheese, sold fresh or aged. Among its most popular aged forms is pecorino romano from Rome and its vicinity.

Provolone Pale yellow, fairly firm cheese made from cow's or water buffalo's milk. Its flavor ranges from mild and slightly sweet to strong and tangy.

Ricotta A light, mild and soft fresh cheese traditionally made from sheep's milk, although cow's milk ricotta is far more common today. For the best quality, seek out fresh ricotta, found in Italian delicatessens; good ricotta may also be sold in small tubs in most markets.

Taleggio A cow's milk cheese from Lombardy, appreciated for its soft, smooth texture and a taste that ranges from slightly piquant to strong depending upon age.

Eggplants
Tender, mildly earthy, sweet vegetable-fruits covered with tough, shiny skin, which may be peeled or left on in grilled or long-cooked dishes. Eggplants vary in color from the familiar purple to red and from yellow to white. The most common variety is the large, purple globe eggplant (above right), but many markets also carry the slender, purple Asian variety, which is more tender

and has fewer, smaller seeds. Also known as *aubergine* and in Italy as *melanzana*.

Garlic
This intensely aromatic bulb has helped to define the character of Italian cooking since ancient times. To ensure the best flavor, buy whole heads of dry garlic, separating individual cloves from the head as needed, and do not purchase more than you will use in 1 or 2 weeks.

TO PEEL A GARLIC CLOVE
Place the clove on a work surface and cover it with the side of a large knife. Press down firmly but carefully on the side of the knife to crush the clove slightly; the skin will slip off easily. Then, slice or mince the clove as required.

Green Lentils
Among the green varieties of this small, disk-shaped dried legume, the French Puy lentil, from the Auvergne town of Le Puy, is considered one of the finest. As with beans, pick over lentils carefully to remove impurities or shriveled lentils before cooking.

Herbs
A wide variety of fresh and dried herbs add complex character to pizzeria dishes. Some popular varieties include:

Basil A sweet, spicy herb used both dried and fresh in pesto and tomato sauces, pizza toppings and calzone fillings.

Chives Long, thin, fresh green shoots of the chive plant have a mild flavor that recalls the onion, a close relative.

Oregano An herb with an aromatic, spicy flavor that intensifies with drying. Also known as wild marjoram.

Parsley Although this popular fresh herb is available in two varieties, Italian cooks prefer flat-leaf parsley, also known as Italian parsley, which has a more pronounced flavor than the curly-leaf type.

Rosemary Used fresh or dried, strong-flavored rosemary frequently scents focaccia, poultry and vegetables.

Sage Fresh or dried, this pungent herb seasons focaccia, beans, meat and poultry.

Thyme Delicately fragrant and clean tasting, this small-leaved herb is used fresh or dried to flavor a wide variety of savory dishes.

Mortadella
A specialty of Bologna, this wide, mottled pork sausage has a mildly spicy flavor and a fine texture that make it a suitable ingredient in pizza toppings and other pizzeria

recipes. Traditionally, the meat was ground in a special "mortar for pig's meat," or *mortaio per carne di maiale,* from which the name of the sausage is derived.

Mushrooms
With their rich, earthy flavors and meaty textures, mushrooms are regularly featured on pizzas and in other pizzeria fare. Some types used in this book include:

Cremini Similar in size and shape to common cultivated white mushrooms, this variety has a more pronounced flavor and a rich brown skin concealing creamy tan flesh.

Shiitake Meaty in flavor and texture, these Asian mushrooms have flat, dark brown caps 2–3 inches (5–7.5 cm) in diameter.

White These common cultivated mushrooms come in three sizes, from the smallest, or button, to cup, to the largest, or flat mushrooms.

Nuts
A wide variety of nuts figure in both savory and sweet pizzeria dishes. Some featured in this book include:

Almonds Popular oval nuts with a mellow, sweet flavor.

Hazelnuts These spherical nuts, also known as filberts, have a special affinity for chocolate, and are often teamed with it in Italian sweets.

Pine Nuts Often referred to by their Italian name, *pinoli,* these small, ivory nuts, the seeds of a species of pine tree, have a rich, resinous flavor that enhances pesto sauce and pizza toppings.

Walnuts These distinctively crinkled nuts have a rich taste and a crisp texture that complement both savory and sweet dishes. The most familiar variety is the English walnut. The American black walnut, usually sold as shelled pieces, has a stronger flavor.

Olive Oil
Olive oil predominates in the cooking of Italy's warmer regions, from the Ligurian coast and Tuscany southward. Prized for its distinctive fruity flavor, extra-virgin olive oil is extracted from olives on the first pressing without use of heat or chemicals. Olive oil labeled "pure" is less aromatic and flavorful and is often used for general cooking purposes.

Olives
In Italy, particularly in the more southerly regions with harsher soil, olive trees thrive. Ripe black and underripe green olives in varied sizes are cured in combinations of salt, seasonings, brines, oils and vinegars to produce a wide range of piquant and pungent results. The popular Greek Kalamatas are ripe olives that have been cured in brine and are packed in vinegar.

Moroccan olives are ripe fruits that have first been dried in the sun, then packed in oil.

Onions
Many different onion varieties contribute pungent flavor to pizzeria dishes. For general purposes, use common, brown-skinned yellow onions. When sweet yellow onions are called for, select those grown in and labeled after Vidalia, Georgia; Walla Walla, Washington; or Maui, Hawaii. Green onions, also known as scallions or spring onions, are an immature variety whose bulbs have not yet developed and are eaten green tops and all. Red, or Spanish, onions have a flesh tinged bright purple-red and tend to be sweeter than regular onions.

Pancetta
This unsmoked bacon is cured simply with salt and pepper. Available in Italian delicatessens and specialty-food stores, it may be sold flat, although it is commonly available sliced from a large sausage-shaped roll.

Pasta
Italy's best-known staple, pasta is a common addition to the menus of many pizzerias. Among the scores of pasta shapes and varieties available, three of the most common, used in this book, are:

Lasagna Broad, flat noodles with straight or ruffled edges, usually layered with cheese, sauce and other ingredients, then baked. For convenience,

some cooks purchase "no-boil" lasagna noodles, which have been precooked and redried, allowing them to be layered for baking directly from the package.

Linguine Literally, "little tongues," describing the shape in cross section of these long, slightly flattened strands.

Orecchiette Bite-sized pasta shaped like "ears."

Pizza Peel
This wide, flat wooden spatula, with a square, thin-edged wooden blade measuring 24 inches (60 cm) or more in diameter, is a useful tool for sliding pizzas into and out of the oven.

Prosciutto
A specialty of Parma, this raw ham is cured by dry-salting for 1 month, then air-drying in cool curing sheds for 6 months or longer. Used as an ingredient, it is also served as an antipasto, cut into tissue-thin slices that highlight its deep pink color and intense flavor.

Radicchio
The most common variety of this type of chicory has small

reddish purple leaves with creamy white ribs, formed into a sphere. Radicchio may be used in pizza toppings or served raw in salads. Also called red chicory.

Salt
Coarse-grained salt adds a robust crunch of briny taste to focaccia toppings and other pizzeria dishes in which it is included. Cooks can choose from coarse sea salt, which is extracted by evaporation from seawater and has a more pronounced flavor than regular table salt, and kosher salt, a flaked variety that contains no additives and has a somewhat milder flavor than regular table salt.

Sausages, Fresh
Fresh sausages are frequently used for topping pizzas, as well as for serving as a main course. Sweet Italian pork sausages, popular in northern Italy, have a mild flavor and are sometimes seasoned with fennel seed or orange zest. Seek out, as well, the many innovative fresh sausages available in markets today, including those made from chicken or duck, which may be substituted for sweet pork sausage.

Shallots
These small cousins of the onion have a papery brown skin, purple-tinged flesh and a flavor resembling both sweet onion and garlic.

Shrimp

Before cooking, fresh shrimp (prawns) are usually peeled and their thin, veinlike intestinal tracts removed.

TO PEEL AND DEVEIN FRESH SHRIMP

Use your thumbs to split open the thin shell between the legs, then carefully peel it away. With a small, sharp knife, make a shallow slit along the back to expose the veinlike, usually dark intestinal tract. Using the tip of the knife or your fingers, lift up and pull out the vein.

Spinach

Popular in Italy for almost a thousand years, spinach figures in soups, pasta doughs and salads and as a filling for antipasti and calzone.

TO PREPARE SPINACH

For the best results, select smaller, more tender leaves. To remove the tough stems and ribs from mature leaves, fold each leaf in half with its glossier side in, then grasp the stem and pull it toward the leaf tip, peeling it and any prominent ribs away from the leaf. Place the spinach leaves in a sink or basin filled with cold water. Swish the leaves vigorously in the water to remove the dirt. Then lift them out, drain the sink or basin, and rinse it thoroughly. Repeat until no grit remains.

Tomatoes

Introduced from the New World to Italy in the mid-16th century, tomatoes were not popular in Italian kitchens until the 18th century. Today, they find their way into every course of a pizzeria meal except dessert, from antipasti and pizza toppings to soups and pasta sauces.

The most familiar tomatoes, and those that offer the best quality year-round, are Italian plum tomatoes, also known as Roma or egg tomatoes.

Canned whole plum tomatoes are the most reliable for cooking; those designated San Marzano are considered the finest. At the peak of summer, also look for little cherry tomatoes and pear-shaped yellow tomatoes, which add intense sweet flavor and bright color to both salads and cooked dishes. Ripe tomatoes are also dried in the sun and preserved in olive oil or packaged dry; the former remain pliant, ready to add to cooked dishes, while the latter require reconstituting by soaking them in cool water.

Vinegars

The term *vinegar* refers to any alcoholic liquid caused to ferment a second time by certain strains of yeast, turning it highly acidic. Vinegars highlight the qualities of the liquid from which they are made. Red wine vinegar has a more robust flavor than vinegar produced from white wine. Balsamic vinegar, a specialty of Modena for centuries, is made from reduced grape juice and is aged and blended for many years in a succession of casks made of different woods and gradually diminishing in size. The result is a tart-sweet, intensely aromatic vinegar.

Zucchini

A squash native to the New World, the slender, cylindrical green zucchini (also known as courgette) long ago found its way into Italian kitchens. Seek out smaller squashes, which have a finer texture and tinier seeds than more mature specimens. Italian cooks who grow zucchini in their own gardens take care to save the delicate blossoms, using them in pasta sauces or stuffing them for an antipasto. In the spring, well-stocked produce markets often sell the squashes with their blossoms still attached.

ACKNOWLEDGMENTS

Evan Kleiman thanks Wendely Harvey, Lisa Atwood and Judith Dunham. She also thanks Kathy Ternay, Brigit Legere Binns and Cindy Mushet for recipe testing and organizational support; the women of The Immaculate Heart Center in Montecito for providing sanctuary; and Oldways Preservation and Exchange Trust for allowing her the opportunity to reexperience the food of southern Italy.

For lending photographic props, the photographer and stylist thank the following:

Accoutrement, Mosman, NSW

Bay Tree, Woollahra, NSW

Art of Food and Wine, Woollahra, NSW

Country Floors, Woollahra, NSW

For their valuable editorial support, the publishers would like to thank:
Desne Border, Ken DellaPenta and Tina Schmitz.

PHOTO CREDITS

Pages 2–3:
Nancy Wasserman/
International Stock
Pages 6–7:
Amanda Merullo/
Stock Boston
Page 8:
David R. Frazier
Page 9:
Susan Lapides (top left)
Steven Rothfeld (bottom right)

Index

PIZZERIA: THE BEST OF CASUAL PIZZA OVEN COOKING